# HOW TO LOVE
YOUR NEIGHBOR

*By the Same Author*

LIVING WITH PURPOSE
YOUR POWER TO BE
THE THIRTEEN COMMANDMENTS
HERE'S A THOUGHT

# HOW TO LOVE YOUR NEIGHBOR

J. SIG PAULSON

DOUBLEDAY & COMPANY, INC.
GARDEN CITY, NEW YORK
1974

The author is grateful to Mrs. Martha Smock for permission to reprint her poem "No Other Way," and to Ann Landers, Publishers-Hall Syndicate and the Kansas City *Star* for permission to use an excerpt from Miss Landers' column.

Some of the material used in this book originally appeared in Unity periodicals and is used by permission of Unity School of Christianity.

Library of Congress Cataloging in Publication Data

Paulson, J    Sig.
    How to love your neighbor.

    1. Love (Theology) 2. Christian life—Unity School of Christianity authors. I. Title.
BV4639.P316    248′.48′99
ISBN 0-385-04263-9
Library of Congress Catalog Card Number 76–89098

Copyright © 1974 by J. Sig Paulson
All Rights Reserved
Printed in the United States of America
First Edition

*Dedication*

This book is happily dedicated to one of the loveliest women in my world, my beautiful daughter, Pam.

## THANK YOU

I am grateful to the men and women, boys and girls all over the world who have given me (and are continuing to give me) lessons in how to love your neighbor.

# CONTENTS

| | | |
|---|---|---|
| I. | The Why of It | 1 |
| II. | Unexpected Beginnings | 4 |
| III. | God Is Love | 8 |
| IV. | What Is Love? | 13 |
| V. | Living in Love | 17 |
| VI. | The Room for Improvement | 24 |
| VII. | Attitudes Are Contagious | 29 |
| VIII. | See God in a New Light | 36 |
| IX. | The Will of God | 41 |
| X. | A New Self-attitude | 44 |
| XI. | Wake Up, Everybody! | 51 |
| XII. | Stirring Up the L-current | 55 |
| XIII. | See Yourself in a New Light | 64 |
| XIV. | Be Yourself | 70 |
| XV. | Loving Your Neighbor | 78 |
| XVI. | Spiritual Independents League | 85 |
| XVII. | Gird Yourself with Love | 93 |
| XVIII. | See Your Neighbor in a New Light | 102 |
| XIX. | Let Your Neighbor Love You | 107 |
| XX. | Develop Your "LQ" | 117 |
| XXI. | The Options of Love | 125 |
| XXII. | Love and Justice | 137 |
| XXIII. | From Adultery to Adulthood | 143 |
| XXIV. | Love and Cosmic Sexuality | 154 |
| XXV. | The Laser Beam of Spirit | 169 |
| XXVI. | Reminders | 173 |
| XXVII. | It Is Finished! | 181 |

# I

# THE WHY OF IT

This is a book I had to write—for the sake of my soul. It all started innocently enough. Alexander Liepa and Maud Savage, of Doubleday & Company, and I were at lunch in New York City when the conversation turned to the possibility of my writing another book. I mentioned the feeling that I had had for several years that I'd like to write something on "How to Love Your Neighbor." Since some of the ideas I shared appealed to Alex and Maud, we agreed that I should undertake the assignment. If I had known what was in store for me, my enthusiasm for the project might have taken a different direction, because this has been part of a soul-shaking experience that is still under way. In the bliss of ignorance, I assumed that I knew something of the nature of love. I had always been surrounded by happy, kind, affectionate, appreciative people—in my family experiences, my work, and my social contacts. Oh, there were temporary rough spots emotionally, but I had seemed to come through them without getting or giving too many scars. I moved in a gentle, mostly harmonious, peaceful world—and if I had been asked, I am sure I would have admitted that I loved God, my neighbor, myself, my family and friends, my coworkers and associates, my work and my world. A pretty smug, snug way of life, you may be thinking. Yes, but in my busy way, I did not realize it. I felt that it would be fairly simple to write a book on love—I knew many definitions of the word, had given countless lessons on the subject, and even written extensively on the ideas and practice of love. Now, several years later, I realize that I know very little about love, and I am only too painfully aware how far I am from really loving anyone, myself included. But I am also grateful and strangely elated because I have caught (like many others) at least an occasional glimpse of the universe of love and the freedom and joy experienced by all who have the courage and faith to enter its creative atmosphere.

So do me a favor, will you please? Read this book and apply the ideas and courses of action that appeal to you with a light heart, a spirit of joy, and a sense of adventure. Even if the creative energy of love on which it is based flows into you with an impact that knocks the electrons off your tight little atoms of living, leaves you startled, gasping, growing, as it has me, let it flow, let it glow, let it grow in intensity. If you are like me, you have probably had enough of the somber, burdensome, unhappy business of trying to reform, convert, save, outwit, outfight, or outwork your neighbor (present world conditions give ample testimony to the bankruptcy of this approach). Let love wake you up, stab you awake, if necessary, inspire you, challenge you, lift your vision of yourself, enrich and change all your relationships, make you a more exciting, romantic, adventurous human being. Let love launch you into the true joy of living; or, if you have already been launched, let love deepen and expand your appreciation of the goodness and wonder of life and all its creatures. Love is the energy that is to govern the world of the future, and right now is the time to link up with it! Experts in the spiritual, medical, and psychological fields assure us we are on the right track, even if we have not reached the final destination!

To love your neighbor is to go beyond the call of duty, the burden of obligation, the narrow codes of convention, the rigid rules of halfliving, into the joy of a new way of life. To prepare to love your neighbor is to take a new and joyous (and often an honest and painful) look at God, yourself, your neighbor, your world, and everything in it.

The most important element in anything you do is your own attitude toward it—so right now, as you begin to read this book, why not take the time to establish the attitude of joy and anticipation in the greatest assignment life has for you, loving your neighbor as yourself. The courses of action described in the

## THE WHY OF IT

following statements may be helpful in shaping your attitude and feeling:

*Reading this book is working a deep and joyous transformation in me.*

*I learn to love my neighbor with growing confidence, joy, enthusiasm, and expectation.*

*I fully expect to enjoy learning to love my neighbor.*

## II

# UNEXPECTED BEGINNINGS

I was beginning to think about starting to write this book when something happened to a good friend of mine that shook me to the roots of my being. This friend had had a successful career and had traveled around the world in his business, meeting people from every walk of life. He had a lovely family, wide interests, and a challenging and inspiring profession. One morning, after returning from an extensive European tour, he tried to get out of bed, and his body refused to obey him. He tried everything he knew, but his body remained inert. Finally, he called his wife and asked her to call a physician friend of his. After listening to the symptoms, the doctor told my friend's wife to call another well-known doctor, who told her to let her husband stay put for a few hours, and then see if he could muster enough strength to come into the office that afternoon.

Later that day, after a thorough examination, the doctor told my friend: "You're a very lucky man on two counts. First, you stopped just on the verge of a serious heart attack; and, second, you have the constitution of a horse. Now, I am going to give you a choice—you can either go to the hospital, or, since you seem to be a fairly intelligent fellow, you can go home and stay in bed for at least three weeks. I want you to take no work home and not even think of your office or business. I want you to read popular books and magazines, watch television—do anything but what you have been doing. In short, I want you to get bored as hell." My friend responded: "Doc, I am bored as hell just listening to you—but I don't want to go to a hospital . . . so I'll follow your instructions."

## UNEXPECTED BEGINNINGS

For the first time in many years, my friend was forced to stop running around the world and take a look at himself. The habitual pattern of his life was disrupted and, almost involuntarily, he became conscious of himself, his relationships, his life style. One night the inevitable crisis came. Let him describe it in his own words: "It was shortly past midnight, and suddenly I could feel the life current in me winding itself down. The strength ebbed out of my body and my heart. I could sense my heartbeat slowing, weakening, almost disappearing. There was no fear, only a deep sense of infinite love and peace and a keen interest in what was happening inside me. (Later, my wife told me she realized what was happening, but knew she was powerless to do anything but pray, for I was on my own, transacting business with my God. Months later, a friend in another part of the country told me that she, too, realized I was going through a crisis at that time.)

"Then a strange thing happened. I began discarding the roles I had been playing, the images I had projected to the world. I saw my husband image dissolve and drop away; my father image, my brother image, my son image, my family image, my social images all dissolved and dropped away; then my business image, my professional image, my work image followed the same pattern and dropped away. I saw the whole pattern of my life dissolving and dropping away, and suddenly I started to laugh because I saw the humor in my whole experience; how seriously I had played those roles; how diligently I had supported and insisted on many things that had seemed so important and essential at the time, but now were being seen in a new perspective. And there I was, stripped naked, shorn of my roles and images, with only my inner self to face the love that had created me.

"I became conscious of my heartbeat again, and I realized that a countdown was under way. Slowly, quietly, inexorably, I could feel myself being moved to the very brink of the abyss—and then I knew that the next heartbeat was crucial. It was up to me to reach a decision—my next heartbeat would be in the visible world, in my body, or it would move me into the invisible realm. My heartbeat would never stop, it would simply be transferred to another dimension of being. Then came a pause, my whole being was hushed—and it seemed that I heard an inner voice saying: 'Stay in the visible realm—you have things to do here.' Immediately strength and life began to flow back into my body, and, according to my doctor, my recovery was phenomenal.

"Soon family and friends were rejoicing and saying, 'Good old ———. He's back to his old self again.' But, of course, 'Good old ———' could never go back to his old self again. Oh, I plugged back into most of the roles to which I had committed myself, but none of them were ever the same again.

"For quite a while I felt like a newborn colt on the Montana plains, trying to pull his legs up under himself so he could stand erect. I felt as if a giant hammer had shattered my self—in fact, I often felt that I had lost my self-identity. I would be in a group and ask myself: 'What am I doing here?' I almost felt that I was beginning a new incarnation, because I looked at everything and everyone in a new light. New emotions kept bubbling up in me. Many of the new feelings were so foreign to me, and often so contrary to conventional and acceptable codes, that I kept them to myself in large measure, realizing that they had to gather strength and stabilize within me. Interestingly, when I returned to my doctor for the final checkup, he said: 'Not only was your healing a phenomenal thing—you're not the man who came in to see me just a few weeks ago.' I realized that changes were taking place deep within me—but we change slowly, don't we? Old habits, old emotions, old patterns, old self hangups do not often just quietly fade away. They have deep roots and a tenacity for self-preservation. 'It's hard for an old rake to turn over a new leaf,' as someone has observed. The old world, both inside and around us, is pretty solidly geared to continue in its old ruts. And so it was that I returned to familiar surroundings, relationships, and work, settling into a fairly comfortable pattern—although there were flashes from within that made me know that something was still going on inside.

"About two and a half years later, I was on a canoe trip to Canada with a friend. We had camped for the night on a bluff overlooking Cache Bay and a tremendous storm came up, at times threatening to blow our entire camp into the bay. At the height of the storm, with rain drenching the tent, flashes of lightning zippering the sky, and thunderbolts colliding everywhere, I became aware of something taking place deep inside me. I saw my old self standing in the depths of me—and he had a message: 'Let me die, or I will kill you.' I watched in amazement—and the message came again: 'Let me die, or I'll kill you.' The message came through in a very quiet, loving, but insistent way—'Let me die and use the energies that support me to bring your new self into being.'"

My friend's experience has moved me pretty deeply, because for over half a century I have been living in, through, and as him. I don't pretend, even to myself, that I have made any great strides in the direction of a new selfhood. The old self has plenty of muscle left, I discover, whenever I try to force the issue or to hasten his dissolution and replacement. On the other hand, a new sense of freedom is constantly asserting itself, and glimpses of a new way of life are popping into consciousness more often and for longer periods. It is clear to me that I am not what I am going to be, but the old state of selfhood is shot pretty full of holes, and perhaps soon I can turn the light of love on him and let him go out in a blaze of glory, as he requested on a stormy night in what seems like several lifetimes ago.

I am concluding that our real growth takes place at levels far below the conscious mind. It is a process generated, sustained, and expanded by the Creator, and it enters our consciousness and gradually (or at times suddenly) takes over in our lives. No doubt it is an eternal process, since each of us is an infinite self or soul unfolding its potentiality—so we all have a long, creative, adventurous journey ahead. I am glad to share some of my experiences with you. They may shed light on some of the inner stirrings of your own soul. I know you have them, because this is the time foretold when "the Spirit (Love) is being poured out on all flesh."

## III

## GOD IS LOVE

The greatest discovery in the long and checkered history of mankind is revealed in these three simple words: "God is love." As humanity accepts and realizes the truth that these words contain, a new race of beings will come forth on this earth. To make it even more specific, as you and I realize the truth that these words contain, we will become new creatures, opening ourselves to a dynamic and creative process of self-unfoldment and expression.

"God is love." Take these words into your being right now. Repeat them aloud to yourself if you are in a spot where you can do this. Taste them with your tongue. Let them flow into your mind. Turn them over. Let them take root in your thought processes. Drop them into your heart. Let them become an integral part of your feeling nature. Let them move in and through your emotions. Open your soul wide to these marvelous words. Let them bring new light to the very roots of your consciousness within you. Let them dissolve and wash away forever all the limited concepts you may have entertained concerning the nature of the Creator. Let them flow into every intelligent and responsive cell of your body. Let the words, the idea they contain, the living truth that they are, take over completely in you.

(This book is not designed to be read at one sitting. When an idea or a course of action described in these pages strikes a responsive note in you, please take the time to lay hold of it, work it into your system of thought and feeling. Let it become an active part of your personal makeup. One idea or revelation of truth—one feeling of love—that becomes activated in you is more important to you and the world than all the truth books, Bibles, and Scriptures resting on library shelves and coffee tables around the globe. No truth, no revelation of the nature of God or of ourselves, is valid for us until it becomes active in our thought, feeling, and expression.)

The words we read and speak are powerful instruments for working in our own being—so perhaps you will be willing to use some of the following statements either in the form presented or as revised by your own consciousness.

*"I am utterly delighted by the discovery and growing realization that God is love!"*

As you use the words, let their activity expand within you. Let them bring up a feeling of delight and rejoicing. Let them stir up your gratitude. Even before you realize fully what these words mean, their rich promise can lift your whole being to a joyous state of expectation.

Following is another thought and feeling process expressed in words that you may wish to accept, adapt, and reshape to your own liking as a process within you.

*"Every time I realize that God is love, I enjoy it more. I do it better, and my understanding of the nature of God is greater, freer, and healthier than ever before."*

If you are really eager to experience the growing power of love in your life, work with these ideas and words, and others that will arise out of your own inner nature, until you really get the feeling of them. You will discover that words and ideas are living units of creative energy, and as they become vital parts of your conscious and subconscious being, you will realize that you are entering a new state of selfhood, a new way of looking at life, at yourself, at your neighbor, at your world. Do everything with a growing sense of joy. Even as you go through some soul-shaking experiences, you will know that there is a deep and abiding joy within you that is constantly growing as the realization that "God is love" becomes a permanent part of you. The nature of the Creator, therefore, the nature of the universe, the nature of every creature is love. So deep and so powerful is this simple message of love that any degree of willing acceptance on your part immediately begins the work of transformation. Love becomes an activity that will grow and unfold until it takes over in mind, heart, body, and affairs. Even a little bit of love activated in an individual will permeate his whole being and his whole world.

"God is love." The impact of this simple truth will eventually change all human experience. It will revolutionize our religion, our politics, our society, our international activities, our whole world. The secret, the mystery, the truth of being is available to anyone. The nature of God, the Creator of the universe, is revealed. Those who are co-operating with the Creator, all who are letting love operate in them, are becoming attuned to the real universe, the universe of truth and life and beauty. Those who know that love is the Creator of the universe know God. Those who do not know this do not know God, and they are out of tune with their own true nature and out of step with the creative process that is bringing mankind into its destiny of freedom and fulfillment.

Take the time daily to do your own thinking and feeling about the nature of God and your growing realization that the Creator is love.

Following are a few ideas and feelings expressed in words that have come to me as I contemplate the marvelous truth that "God is love." I realize that my mind and heart do not operate in exactly the same way yours do, but I am glad to share my growing conclusions with you:

The only version of God, available in the open market today, that appeals to me is this: "God is love." Love is the only God whose image I desire to be. Admittedly, I know very little about love, but what I do know makes me eager to know more.

I believe that God is love simply because I want to believe it. It satisfies the logic of my mind and of my heart. It makes me glad and grateful. It has the "ring" of truth. It pleases me. It satisfies me, and I feel it is important that the nature of God should please and satisfy me. I can joyously believe in, accept, worship, and serve the God of love.

I am eager to believe that God is love because I want a lovable God. The true God must be lovable to man. I have a feeling that

## GOD IS LOVE

I and most of humanity have wasted much energy and time trying to love gods that did not really deserve it! I am choosy about the God in whom I invest my love! And I know you are too. The God of love—pure, changeless, infinite, eternal love—is a lovable God, and I am willing to love that God of love with all my heart, with all my soul, with all my mind, with all my strength, with all that I am.

I am eager to believe that God is love because I want a healthy God. I am tired of the sickly, repugnant, ridiculous gods that men have worshiped in the past. The reported god of anger, punishment, retaliation, and vengeance would make a sick, hateful human being, to say nothing of an impossible creator. If God is our Heavenly Father, as the "good book" indicates, then I want a healthy father, which infinite love is.

I am eager to believe that God is love because I want a healthy, whole humanity. Since we are all members of one family, the children of one heavenly father, then we inherit the divine nature of love, and that love is what makes and keeps us healthy.

I am eager to believe that God is love because I want a good world to emerge from all the struggle and growth that are taking place in it. A good world, call it heaven if you choose, can come only from a good creator, and anything less than infinite love cannot produce it.

I am eager to believe that God is love because I want to be happy, and everyone I know wants to be happy. This desire for joy and happiness must have a source, and only the God of love would give it to man, because in the irresistible creative activity of love, that desire will be fulfilled.

I am eager to believe that God is love because I have experienced enough love in this sojourn on earth to want more of it. This deep desire for love that is present in every human being could come only from a creator whose nature is love—the love that is capable of fulfilling the desire for itself.

I am eager to believe that God is love because men and women in every walk of life—doctors, psychiatrists, psychologists, ministers, counselors, educators, political leaders, workers, housewives

—are recognizing the need for and the ultimate power of love. Surely the Creator is capable of supplying the need of His creation. The time is rapidly coming when "every knee shall bow," every mind will admit, every heart will open, every life will be surrendered to the almighty power of infinite love.

I am eager to believe that God is love because men become like the gods they worship. In a very real sense man is always the image of the god he believes in. When man believes in God as love, then love will govern his attitudes, his thoughts and feelings, his actions and reactions, and his world will change to give expression to that love. It's that simple.

As you ponder the wonder that is love, new and constantly more powerful revelations of its nature will stir within you. Love is so powerful that even words about it work miracles in mind and heart. Thinking about love, opening your awareness to the presence and power of love within you, awaken you to the truth that "God is love." In the process you may find many old concepts of deity boiling up to the surface of your mind. If they do, let them go. You have no further obligation to them, and you need serve them no longer. You are mature enough to be through with childish beliefs, superstitions, concepts, and attitudes. You always have the right to choose the god you worship, and you can "choose this day whom you will serve."

## IV

## WHAT IS LOVE?

Love has been defined in many different ways—from "a many-splendored thing" to "a many-splintered thing," from "sweet mystery of life" to "sweet misery of life," depending upon the definer's most recent experience in the eternal assignment of learning to love. Perhaps one of the best definitions would be "love is God"—that would be defining the undefinable in terms of the undefinable. The moment we begin to define something, we of course confine it in our definitions. Love is self-existent, eternal, and infinite—and it probably can never be defined in terms of anything else. It is its own nature, its own activity, its own expression. There is only one love in the universe, its creator. Every bit of love we have experienced—mother love, family love, friendly love, human affection, love of beauty, work, and world—is a degree and expression of the one love.

While love cannot really be defined, it can be experienced by anyone who is willing to open his mind and heart and being to it. Love is the creative energy in which the whole universe lives and moves and has existence. Love gives life and light to all that is now, all that has ever been, and all that ever will be. We are more familiar with what love does than with what it is, and that's the way it should be, because love is active energy, life itself. We all know from personal experience and observation, and also through the experiences of others, that love heals all manner of diseases, brings a sparkle of life and vitality to the eye and the body of anyone in whom it operates, forgives all sins and shortcomings, keeps no score of wrongs, is patient and kind. It is not jealous or boastful or irritable or resentful, does not rejoice in what is wrong. Love finds pleasure in the truth, fulfills the law, every law, the law of being, the law of our own individual potential and nature. Love wipes out fear, guilt, condemnation, unhappiness, and completely transforms the individual or situation in which it is permitted to operate. You can add to this list many wonderful things of your own that you realize love does—so it is evident, on the basis of experience, that it is important and essential that we become acquainted with love. Each one will start where he is in understanding and consciousness, because the experience of love is individual and unique to each one. Ignorance of the nature of love—that is, the ultimate nature of it—is not a valid reason for us to hold back.

We are also well aware of the unhappy consequences of unloving attitudes and actions. There is no need to enumerate what fear and hatred and guilt and condemnation do. We are all too familiar with the products of non-love to take the time and space to list them.

Modern-day psychiatrists and doctors of the mind and heart say, "Love or perish." Back in the days when men settled their differences by throwing rocks at each other, the disastrous results of unloving attitudes were not quite so readily apparent. In these days of atomic bombs, however, our whole civilization is threatened with destruction unless men learn to love—and quickly. So let nothing come ahead of love.

A wonderful clergyman friend of mine, who retired after more than fifty years in the active ministry of the church, told me that if he had his life work to do over again, he would make love his central theme, even though he did not really know what it is. He said he thought love is so important that he would never preach a sermon on any other subject, and he would encourage his congregation to learn to love. He commented that, even though the early church was known for the love expressed by its members, he had to admit that in the churches where he had served he had seen little evidence of genuine love. "How little," he concluded, "we know of love." We may know little of love, but the only way

## WHAT IS LOVE?

to learn more is to put into practice the knowledge we do have. So let's begin right where we are.

Perhaps you will find the following exercise of benefit as you put into practice the love you already know.

*My growth in the understanding of the nature of love is dependent more on putting into practice the love I already have within me than on more study and definitions. Love is the creative energy (or spirit) in which the whole universe exists. I, too, am a living part of that universe that is brought into being and sustained by love. As I practice the love I already know, my understanding of its nature and power grows constantly.*

Here is another idea that you might add to your practice of love. I have put it into words, but you will be able to translate it into the activity they describe.

*Every time I practice the love I know, I enjoy it more, I do it better, and my understanding of the nature of love is healthier, stronger, and more complete than ever before.*

Discovering the nature of love is an inside work. It is an activity that takes place in your own mind and heart, and it unfolds as new awareness and understanding of the nature of the creative spirit of the universe. Take the time often to become quiet and feel the activity of love within your being. Ask that infinite love to reveal its nature to and through you. Your own research into the nature of love is just as valid as that of anyone who has ever lived. Do not settle for secondhand information about the nature of love in you. Get it firsthand by accepting its presence within you and opening your whole being to its activity.

I want to share with you, as far as words will permit me to do so, elements of the nature of love as they have been revealed to me in my own experience. I like to think of these elements as the gospel of the trinity of creative energy—or the three L's of the creative spirit: LOVE–LIFE–LIGHT. Love is the creative field of energy, or universal spirit, out of which all creation proceeds. Life is the activity of that love. And light is the radiant substance produced by the life activity of love, out of which all creation and its creatures are made. The Creative Spirit (God) is the love, life, and light of creation. This eternal universe of love, life, and light is the divine dwelling place of man. Not only that—love, life, and light are the elements of man's real nature; or, to put it in the words of Jesus Christ, "the kingdom of God is within you." "God is spirit"—love, life, and light—and each individual is in the process of awakening to this inner spiritual nature, which is to be brought into ever greater expression through all of us. Man is created to be the embodier and expresser of the love, life, and light that God is. So you can realize, my wonderful friend, that in coming to know and experience the nature of love we are not engaged in a minor skirmish. We are deepening, broadening, and expanding the foundation of our very existence. We are moving through the transitional experience of dying to our old self and being awakened to, and in, a new selfhood. We are being converted into an entirely different type of creature from the old fearful, guilty, limited, earthbound, selfish product of ignorance that man has been. In the process of discovering the nature and power of love, there will not be a stone unturned in our structure of life. We will be re-created from within, and the energy that will do the work is the divine power of love, life, and light deep within us.

What is love? God is! You are! I am!

As love unfolds its infinite nature through us, we will throb with new life and glow with new light, and we will become the self-expression of infinite love that we are created to be!

## V

## LIVING IN LOVE

As you become more intimately acquainted with love, you will discover that it is a field of pure creative spiritual energy in which all creation lives and moves and has being. It is in reality the dwelling place of your own soul and the eternal dwelling place of all humanity. Love is also the current of divine energy that animates your being and finds its self-expression in and through you. The New Testament tells of the nature of love simply, accurately, and beautifully: "God is love, and the man whose life is lived in love does in fact live in God, and God does in fact live in him." Jesus Christ also pointed out to those who would follow him: "You must go on living in my love. If you keep my commandments you will live in my love just as I have kept my Father's commandment and live in His love."

"God is love," and that love is our true home, our dwelling place, the divine presence, the creative atmosphere in which we are designed to live. It is not a physical place. It is in fact the ocean of invisible creative energy in which all manifest (physical) creation floats and lives. Love surrounds, contains, sustains, and animates you—and everything else in the universe. Love is the "Garden of Eden" on which Adam and Eve lost their lease when they permitted the sense of sin, guilt, and shame to come between them and the Creator. The allegorical story of Adam and Eve in the Old Testament applies to all of us. What keeps man from returning to the "Garden," the paradise he naturally seeks, is his sense of sin, guilt, and shame, which holds him in a world of limitation, burden, condemnation, and separation. The block that keeps man from paradise is not in God, the love that "keeps no score of wrongs," but in man—in his false beliefs, his distorted concepts, his fearful patterns of thought, feeling, and action. In spite of the efforts of all "saviors," including Jesus Christ, most of humanity is stubbornly hanging on to the obstacles that block entry into the paradise it seeks.

Love has been man's dwelling place throughout all the generations of his soul, through every experience of living and growing, although, for the most part, man has not known or believed or accepted it. Love is the healing, freeing, saving presence that draws men to its grace and wholeness that they might become what they are created to be—love in self-expression. Eventually, all men are to enter the eternal dwelling place of love and stay there—to live in it and to live from it.

Regardless of the state of mind a person happens to be in, he is free to start the journey into the dwelling place of love through a simple verbal/mental process. He can take words that describe the course of action he wishes to initiate within himself and, as he thinks about the activity the words describe and gets the feeling of the activity, he will be moved more closely and deeply into that eternal dwelling place. Eventually, of course, the words dissolve into the activity they describe; then the whole procedure becomes silent and even more powerful. The course of action described in the following words will move you more deeply into the kingdom and experience of love:

*God is love. That infinite love is my rightful dwelling place. Love is drawing me into its healing, freeing, saving presence. I am designed to live, move, and have my being in love. I relax and let love take over. I am grateful that love surrounds, contains, animates, and sustains me.*

Words are important. Words of love stir the dullest mind and inspire the heaviest heart. When you realize that the words you use are part of a mental, emotional, spiritual process, they become even more effective in your own experience. On the other hand, do not remain too closely tied to them. Enter the process they describe even as you think, read, and/or speak them. Love is the eternal presence that surrounds you, and even the slightest mental and verbal move on your part brings an immediate response from the divine energy or spirit that yearns for you as deeply as you yearn for it. Love rushes to meet and greet you as you turn to it in faith and joyous anticipation. Realize that you are not just reading another book (unless you *are* just reading another book!). Love in you, and love through the words of this book, is inviting you to enter consciously into its dynamic presence, to be filled with its throbbing, vital life current, to be aglow with its light in this creative and adventurous age. Nobody has time just to write another book, or just to read another book. Every activity, every encounter, is part of an awakening of the soul to its living place in love.

Enjoy the process of returning to love, your eternal dwelling place. You are engaged in the most important activity taking place on earth. You are coming to know and experience a creative energy that is to govern the new generation of men, a new race being brought forth in the world. You are tapping the dynamic power that is bringing an old civilization to an end and laying the foundation for its successor. And to make it very personal and specific, you are tapping the dynamic power that is bringing an old state of selfhood to an end and laying the foundation for its successor in you. The spirit of love is being poured out on all flesh and into every mind and heart, regardless of appearances. All humanity is about to get what it so richly deserves and desperately needs—the love that is God!

Love is a most unusual dwelling place. Those who want to live in it find they have to give up many of their personal possessions. In the days of the Old West in the United States, cowboys were not permitted to enter church with their guns on but had to leave them outside until after the services, when they were allowed to pick them up again. Love is a much holier place than any church; one has only to set foot on the porch of this divine dwelling place to learn that he must begin to set aside most of his human arsenal of attitudes, thoughts, and feelings. Love strips the one who would enter its wholesome, vigorous atmosphere "naked as a jaybird." "For the word that God (Love) speaks is alive and active: it cuts more keenly than any two-edged sword: it strikes through to the place where soul and spirit meet, to the innermost intimacies of a man's being: it exposes the very thoughts and motives of a man's heart. No creature has any cover from the sight of God (Love); everything lies naked and exposed before the eyes of Him with whom we have to do" (Hebrews 4:12–13, Phillips).

If you have believed that love is weak, passive, and ineffective, even a short stay in its vibrant presence will soon awaken you to the truth that it is the most powerful, dynamic, and creative energy in the universe. Electricity, atomic energy, light, and even life are only its radiations. Love is the energy that is to make a new creature out of you (and me)—and that's no small undertaking!

Love penetrates to the depths of the one who has the faith and audacity to live in it. It moves immediately to take away what is in him of impatience, unkindness, envy, possessiveness, boastfulness, conceit, rudeness, selfishness, touchiness, and other elements of self-concern. It even strips him of his record of personal sins, shortcomings, limitations, and alibis. It silences his childish excuses and makes a man out of him. It clears his vision and brings to his remembrance the great truth that he is its chosen instrument of self-expression. It dissolves fear—fear of punishment, fear of failure, fear of success, fear of fear. It wipes out burdens of guilt, condemnation, inertia, and procrastination, and moves the one living in it to inspired mental, emotional, and physical action. Living in love is no minor project. If you are sincere about it, you are headed for a completely new way of life and a new selfhood.

If you are ready for it, immerse yourself in the love that is your true dwelling place and let your old sense of selfhood, with its arsenal of protective hardware, be dissolved. The process that accelerates your move into love can be described in words like the following:

*God is love. I move into that love now, and in the light of love I am stripped of all my defense mechanisms and excuses for self-limitation. I rejoice as love strips the gravecloths of fear, selfishness, condemnation, and alibis from my soul and leaves me naked and even shivering. I confidently expect to be reclothed in the garment love has prepared for me.*

Love has no record of man's mistakes and shortcomings. It is too pure to hang on to evil. It delights in the truth of man's infinite potential. There is no condition, circumstance, or sin that love cannot face and handle triumphantly. There is no limit to its faith, its power, or, in man, its self-expression. There is no limit to its hope, its desire for self-expression through man, coupled with the expectation of attainment. There is no limit to its endurance or staying power. Love is finishing the job of creation, regardless of what man might think at certain stages of his unfoldment. Love is fulfilling all the prophecies it has inspired in man. Love is surpassing the promises of good that the most enlightened of men have accepted and passed on to their fellow men. Love in reality is going far beyond any knowledge we have of it now, for it is infinite. Love is moving and growing man out of childish fears, superstitions, outlooks, thoughts, habits, and ways of life, and making him whole, the image of the Creator. Love is clearing up the puzzling reflections, the distorted vision in man by bringing him face to face with God, with himself, and with his neighbor. Love is fulfilling all the laws of the universe and the law of each individual's potential. Love is wiping out the guilt-edged state of mind in which man has struggled and is revealing his true identity as a glorious son of the Infinite. Love is the dynamic, creative, spiritual energy that keeps the whole universe, including man, alive and growing, moving forward and upward in great cycles and spirals of fulfillment. As you enter consciously more deeply into the dwelling place of love, you will become aware of these great currents of energy that are integrating you into the cosmic plan of creation and stirring up the vision of your potential as a self-expression of infinite love.

The path to living in love has its challenging, as well as joyful, moments and experiences. Love is a persistent God—there is no limit to its activity. It probes into the depths of one willing to live in it. As love continues its work in you, you may find that it leads you to deep questions and hard decisions. The road to living in love is straight and narrow, and among the few who have found it there has been only a small percentage willing to go all the way. Each one who would live in love finds from personal experience that love insists that he be honest with himself, and that is quite a project. Often love corners him in some quiet room in the heavenly dwelling place and he has to ask himself penetrating questions like the following:

"Do I really want to live in love?"

"Am I willing to give up impatience, unkindness, jealousy, possessiveness, boasting, conceit, rudeness, selfishness, touchiness, alibis, excuses?"

"Do I really want to give up my record of personal sins and mistakes, memories they have established, habits of thought and feeling they have become? Or do I want to keep rehearsing them, continuing to see myself as a great sinner and sufferer?"

"Am I ready to stop gloating over or talking about other men's sins, mistakes, and shortcomings?"

"Am I ready to give up fear, resentment, irritation? Do I really want to face myself as I am right now, and let the faith, hope, and enduring power of love make me a new creature?"

"Do I really want to give up my old identity, with its mental, emotional, and physical patterns and be reborn, become a new person? Am I willing to expand and improve outer areas of my life—work, business, relationships, religious or social connections, or even to leave some of them, if necessary?"

"Do I really want to grow up, to leave behind childish and immature beliefs, actions, superstitions, and reactions?"

"Am I ready for a new selfhood, or am I just stirring things up a bit before settling again into my old style of life?"

(Each of us is an individual and travels his own way, so I realize that your questions may take a somewhat different route. On the other hand, I find it helpful to discover what is going on in other persons and check it out against what I am experiencing. It makes me feel that I am part of the human race, and lifts my heart when the going and growing are a bit rough.)

## LIVING IN LOVE

Living in love leads an individual to a state of honesty that is more than merely confessing his sins and shortcomings. Love insists that we confess our potential as its self-expression and begin to think and feel in a new way. This type of honesty leads to questions that demand even more creative, dynamic, and adventurous answers. As love cleans up the old poisonous, limiting, fearful, guilty states of mind and heart, you may find yourself confronted with questions like the following:

"Am I really willing to live up to my potential?"

"Am I willing to be as loving, as alive, as radiant as I am capable of being?"

"Am I willing to be as forgiving, as understanding, as free as love itself?"

Here again you will be having your own experiences. Love operates in and through you in an original, individual, creative way that is unique. There is no duplication in the kingdom of love. Love is freeing you from the old states of negation and limitation, and even from that which you conceive to be good and true, in order that the infinitely greater potential that you are may find expression.

A person who is willing to continue living in love, who answers the deep questions that love inspires in him in a way that keeps him growing, finds a subtle and often spectacular change taking place in his attitudes and feelings. From time to time, he will feel a delightful sense of freedom, as if the burdens of a lifetime or several lifetimes had been lifted from his soul. And that is exactly what is happening. Love does not sit in the judgment seat. It does not add to the burdens of the soul. Love neither condemns nor condones. If it judges, it judges accurately: Every man is a soul or self of the Infinite, and regardless of its present condition, it is capable of responding to the unlimited faith, hope, and staying power of love. Love always acts immediately to heal, free, rejuvenate, resurrect its sons and daughters, regardless of the situation they may be in when they turn to it.

## VI

# THE ROOM FOR IMPROVEMENT

The greatest room in the universe is the room for improvement. I can readily see that the greatest room in my world and in my being is the room for improvement. It is absolutely without limitation. There is no end to it. As one becomes conscious of the activity of love in his being, the desire for improvement becomes joyously irresistible. Love wipes out fear, guilt, and condemnation, and as this inner smog is lifted, the soul is inspired to move audaciously toward freedom from old states of bondage. Old attitudes, and the concepts and false images that produced them, are wiped out. A fresh breeze blows through the corridors of mind and heart, and one who is becoming even slightly conscious of the nature of love finds that he is impelled to question the authority figures of both the inner and outer world with growing confidence, joy, and enthusiasm. Like many others who are discovering that love is the reality of the universe, I found an almost irresistible desire to laugh at the images of God, myself, and others that I had supported so diligently most of my life.

As the nature of love continued to expand its activity in my consciousness, I found my trinity of creative energy—love, life, light—expanded into the four-square gospel of love, life, light, and laughter. I could not help it. The more I looked at the old states of limitation through the eyes of love, the more I laughed at them and the more I laughed at myself for ever holding them. It seemed that everywhere I looked in my inner and outer world, love was lifting the lid off some ridiculous state of limitation and inviting me to laugh myself free from it.

## THE ROOM FOR IMPROVEMENT

This laughter, or deep and abiding joy, seems to be a quality that the prober into love finds within himself. The greatest room in the universe, the room for improvement in love, is filled with shouts of laughter, the delightful sound of deep joy, as hypnotic bonds of false belief are dissolved and cast off. It reminds me of the story I heard about a distinguished scientist who greeted each new discovery of truth with a joyous shout: "Of course, it must be so. It couldn't be otherwise!"

I remember once in a little wooded chapel I had a timeless meditation that was mostly wave after wave of silent laughter and irresistible joy welling up within me. I heard an inner voice saying, "That was one of the best meditations you ever had, wasn't it?" I agreed wholeheartedly with my inner self and then went about the day's activities. The experience brought to mind those words of Jesus to the effect that, if we followed Him far enough, His joy would be in us and our joy would be made full.

This does not mean that there are always times of unalloyed joy on the pathway of love. There are plenty of tears, both inner and outer, in learning to love. At least this has been my experience and the experience of most of those who have shared with me events of their own awakening in love. But in spite of the tears and some of the rougher aspects of the housecleaning that love generates in us, joy is the predominating element. It becomes such a deep, vital, and permanent realization that, no matter what storms of negation seem to be taking place in and around one, a deep, abiding awareness of joy is present. And somehow one realizes that these "things have come to pass."

As you read the words in this book, you will undoubtedly become aware of feelings, energy flows, revelations deep within yourself that you realize are beyond the power of words to convey. This is one book I wish I could write without words. But then, too, I realize this incredible world of love that is opening and awakening in both of us utilizes every element to achieve its goal, and even words on a printed page emit a radiation capable of stirring a response in another's mind and heart and life. Years of experience in speaking and writing have taught me that no one really listens to what I say or reads what I am writing, but the words I speak or write may well deepen and expand a revelation that is already taking place in the listener or reader. In a wonderful way we are both on the same frequency of love, or you wouldn't be reading what I am writing.

An important thing to realize is that it is only your own experience in love that is valid and real for you. Anyone else's experience, no matter how wonderful and valid for him, is a secondhand experience for you. So enter the room for improvement that is the love center of your own being often. Let the feeling and the revelation of love become active in your consciousness, and you will find that what is taking place verifies the experience recorded in the great scriptures and other writings of the world. But never let the revelation of another put a ceiling on your own experience, because you are designed and destined to go beyond any outer scripture into your own realization and experience in love. You are love's divine original—never forget that!

Following is a technique I have found helpful in entering the room for improvement (you may wish to call it your secret chamber). If it "rings a bell" in you, at least start with it and then let it unfold as your own unique experience.

Initially, go into your outer room of meditation or prayer or aloneness—later on, you will find that you can do it on a busy subway or on a crowded street or in an office—and hold the word LOVE in your mind and heart. Simply repeat the word mentally, emotionally, and verbally, either silently or audibly, and let what naturally takes place take place. What you will be doing is setting up a vibration that is really an emanation from the invisible universe of love in which you live and move and have your being, whether you are conscious of it or not. Simply stay with the process for a while without attempting to impose any specific pattern on what you are doing. (I remember once during such an experience that the inner voice came to me saying, "Stop trying to tell me what I am and I'll show you.")

(If you wish to find more detailed instructions on how to stir

## THE ROOM FOR IMPROVEMENT

up love and other powers of being, you may wish to refer to my earlier book *Your Power to Be*.)

As you continue this exercise in love, I can joyously predict that many wonderful things will take place within you. You will be tenderized from within as the current of love (its elements of love, life, light, and laughter) is released into all your systems of self-expression. At times you may feel an almost overwhelming sense of oneness with all creation and a deep appreciation for every living creature, and everything in the universe comes alive in love. Or you may feel a joy so exquisite that it is almost unbearable to your awakening self. At other times you may become conscious of all the pain, the agony, and the despair in human consciousness—but this will not be in a negative sense, because you will realize somehow that, even in the depth of human frustration and darkness, there is the spark of love that can never be quenched.

Do not be discouraged if something spectacular does not take place the first time you enter this type of experience. I am trying to distill into a relatively few words experiences that span not only a lifetime on this glorious earth, but that have roots in the unthinkable eons of total human experience of the past. On the other hand, you may well have brought to your conscious awareness experiences of your own that have gone far beyond anything I am attempting to describe. I know you are an absolutely unlimited being and that fantastic realizations and experiences will begin to unfold in you as you move ever more deeply into the secret place of love, which is the greatest room for improvement in all creation.

After such an experience I like to describe to myself in words a feeling, a desire, a growing realization: Every time I enter the greatest room in my universe, the room for improvement, that secret place of love within my being, I enjoy it more, I do it better, and my understanding of the nature of love is deeper, more creative, and powerful than ever before.

## HOW TO LOVE YOUR NEIGHBOR

What starts out as just statements or words can develop into a powerful realization because we are dealing with the most dynamic and creative energy in the universe—the love that created it.

# VII

# ATTITUDES ARE CONTAGIOUS

The most important element in our living experience is the image we hold of God, the picture we have accepted or developed of the Creator of the universe. Whether we are conscious of it or not, this image of the Infinite is the foundation of our life. It colors our thoughts and our feelings. It makes us courageous, dynamic, creative individuals; or, if it is extremely negative, it makes us weaklings, cowards, ineffective human beings. It shapes our attitudes toward the creative power, toward ourselves, and toward our neighbors.

I will be forever grateful to the woman who handed me a slip of paper after a lecture one evening. On it she had written, "Attitudes are contagious. Is yours worth catching?" Truly our attitude toward God, our Creator, is contagious. Everything in our world (our mind, heart, soul, the cells and organs in our body, our relationships), the entire universe, for that matter, catches our attitude toward God. In this scientific age when researchers are discovering that the universe is so sensitive that one cannot observe it without influencing it, we can readily understand that our attitude toward the source of all things is inevitably transmitted to all the elements of creation. We can appreciate, in ever-increasing measure, the importance of our attitude toward God, our image of the Creator.

Perhaps you'd like to try a little exercise that has both its physical and imaginative elements. This exercise came to me after a discussion I had with the late Dr. Donald Hatch Andrews, professor emeritus of chemistry of Johns Hopkins University, on the sensitivity of the universe. Just raise one of your fingers and wiggle it, and then realize in a very real sense that you are tickling every atom in the universe. (And I might add, as I do often when I ask a group of people to share in this experience, "and every Eve, too!") Dr. Andrews told me that probers into the atomic nature of the universe have discovered that it is so incredibly sensitive that a man cannot move a hand or a finger without changing the relationship of every atom in the universe to every other atom in the universe. He told me that if a man or woman opens his or her lips to speak and one could see what was happening, he would realize that from the speaker's lips there is a current of energy flowing into the universe to become a living and vital part of it. If this happens when a physical movement takes place, think of what occurs when the mind and heart of an individual exercises an attitude or improves one. If this whole experience we have just shared seems incredible to you, my only suggestion is this: Relax and enjoy it, because learning to love is one incredible experience after another.

Probably for most people their attitude toward God is secondhand. It has been shaped by preachers, teachers, parents, society, and is often the product of superstition, ignorance, fear, and guilt. At one time it was pretty common religious practice to "put the fear of God" into the members of various religious groups, and indeed into all humanity, if possible. While there still seem to be some religious systems that hold this attitude, it is wonderful to note that more and more individuals and groups are interested in calling forth the "love of God" that is present, at least potentially, in every person. Since even a reasonably mature human being would not want his children to fear or be afraid of him, it is inconceivable that the Creator of this beautiful universe would seek to instill fear into the human family as an attitude of mind and heart.

You may wish to examine your own attitudes toward God, or whatever name you give to the Creative Spirit, in order that you may have a look at the most important element in your own being and life. Some people have told me that they weren't really

## ATTITUDES ARE CONTAGIOUS

concerned about God, because that was the church's or religion's business, and they were willing to leave it to the priests and the ministers and the authorities in the religious scene. Since you are reading this book, I doubt that you have such an approach to the matter, and I feel that you will be willing to probe into the deep recesses of your being to find out what is going on there.

Following is a format, or an exercise in words, that will enable you to go as deeply as you choose into these basic attitudes. After you have read the words, you may wish to set the book aside and initiate the inner action that the words describe.

*My attitude toward God (Creator) is————. This attitude is contagious, and it influences all the elements and relationships of my life.*

Take as much time as necessary to get under way on this practice. Your inner attitudes toward your Creator exert a tremendous influence in your whole world, and it is only reasonable and wise that you discover what those attitudes are. No doubt there will be some healthy and constructive ones as well as some you will wish to dissolve immediately, depending upon your past experiences, educational training, and other factors. Just taking a look at these attitudes will in itself often prove to be a healing and freeing experience.

If you are a member of the younger generation, you will, in all likelihood, not have so many attitudes to unlearn as we who have been on this earthly scene for a longer period of time. In any event, carrying out and expanding this exercise will give you some practice in self-mastery and a greater feeling for what it really means. Old attitudes of a negative variety, especially if they have been charged with and established in powerful emotions of fear and resentment, are not always easy to overcome—but eventually you will have to overcome and release them, so now is just as good a time as any to get started.

After you have had an opportunity to release some of the attitudes that have bound you, you may wish to begin the process of installing some new ones. The exercise outlined in the following words can be helpful in this project:

*I now adopt a loving, healthy, creative, adventurous attitude toward God, the Creative Spirit. This attitude is also contagious, and I rejoice as it exerts an ever-widening influence in my whole being and world.*

It is undoubtedly wiser to keep what you are doing pretty much to yourself. If, however, you open your mind and your mouth at the wrong time and place and to the wrong person, don't let yourself be bulldozed by the opinions of others. You are entitled to frame your own attitudes, to dissolve those that no longer have validity in your own experience, and to continue on your path of learning the lesson of love.

Just in case you run into some snags, following is what we might call an affirmation, or at least an affirmative approach, that I have found helpful in whatever degree of self-realization I have attained:

*I am neither elated nor deflated by the opinions of others. I am true to the growing integrity of my own soul. I am mature enough to establish, hold, and unfold the dynamic new attitudes I choose for myself.*

If we allow some windbag state of consciousness to come along and inflate our ego balloon, we can be certain that in a short time a pinhead state of consciousness will come along to prick and deflate it. Right now is a good time, in fact the best time in eternity, to learn to trust our inner spirit of truth and our own right and growing ability to choose the attitudes by which we will live. Regardless of how authoritative, formidable, and loudly phrased others' opinions are, there is no time like the present to make the break that moves us on the pathway of self-freedom.

Of course, old attitudes and concepts and opinions are not always presented through other people. They often boil up from deep within the subconscious levels of our being, where they have taken root and grown strong, fat, and comfortable through the years of our lifetimes. They don't always like to be disturbed but would prefer to maintain things pretty much as they are, even though they are painful and self-destructive.

A number of people have told me that they have made what seemed like good starts on the path to self-realization and the freeing of themselves from old binding attitudes, but they discovered that the inner and outer pressures were too much for them. Others have asked me if they could try a new attitude and thought and still maintain their membership, as it were, in old attitudes and concepts just in case these were right, and they had to answer for new, revolutionary attitudes and ideas on the day of final judgment. Each one who is really seeking self-mastery will have to reach these decisions for himself. If he is unwilling or unable to do so, then perhaps it is just as well he move on to other pursuits, and return to the room for improvement in love when he is ready to do so, as inevitably he will become.

My own experience in changing attitudes toward the Creator began explosively and painfully at a rather early age. I had been vigorously exposed to a "hellfire and brimstone" set of attitudes, and while I avoided exposure diligently and as often as I could, occasionally I would be trapped and I would discover that my attitude toward the God that was being preached to me was anything but loving, healthy, creative, and adventurous. In fact, I developed an active dislike for that picture of the Creator, and on one occasion, when the picture was presented a bit more vividly than usual, I could contain myself no longer. I said, in words that were probably neither loving, nor gentle, nor wise, that if that was the true nature of God, I would rather do business with the devil. I could at least trust the devil. He was a stinker all the time, but I just could not accept a god who is sometimes presented as loving and forgiving and understanding and at other times as wrathful, vindictive, vengeful, and cruel beyond comprehension. If there were such a god, I ventured bravely, I wouldn't touch him with a ten-foot pole. I was assured by well-meaning friends, including some ministers, that I had committed the unforgivable sin and would undoubtedly find a reservation in one of the hottest spots in the hell that was bound to come. But my stand was taken, and there was no retreating.

Inevitably, a violent reaction took place, and for a period of six months I was probably the most frightened boy on the face of the earth. I had the awful feeling that every time I walked around the corner the heavens would open and a bolt of lightning would strike me dead. I was on my own. I had no one to share my feelings with. I was taking some uncertain and wavering steps toward self-mastery and realization, and somehow I found or was given the courage to persist. Eventually the turmoil and fear dissolved and I realized, at least vaguely, that I was contending not with an outer power or force, but with inner attitudes and images I had accepted. Throughout my lifetime, remnants of these old attitudes have surfaced and dissolved, and a growing sense of inner freedom has developed.

Just a few years ago I had a dream in which I saw a whole group of darkly clad, heavily robed figures who shook menacing fingers at me, and I had the feeling in the dream that they represented some of the elements out of my past. As I watched, I saw the light in back of and around the figures becoming ever brighter, and suddenly the dark-hooded robes collapsed and fell on the ground and I saw that they were empty. I had no difficulty figuring out the significance of this dream. I realize I have a long way to go before attaining total inner freedom, but at least I recognize that the process is under way.

A few years ago I met a wonderful man in Europe who told me he too had had experiences of this kind. Once when he was a teen-ager he heard a particularly violent "hellfire and brimstone" sermon. He rushed out of the hall, hurried home and knelt by the side of the bed in his room. Out of his inner agony and turmoil he prayed: "Oh, God, if there is such a place as this hell I heard preached tonight, and even one of your children goes there, let me go too, so he will not have to be alone."

He told me that somehow deep in his heart he had always known that God is love and that the fear and hatred and vengeance preached in his name were the product of man's imagination and ignorance.

## ATTITUDES ARE CONTAGIOUS

Someone has observed that God created man in His image, and ever since then man has been trying to return the compliment. A god fabricated out of superstition, ignorance, and hatred has no right to and cannot generate a loving, healthy, creative, and adventurous attitude in human hearts and minds. But the true God, whose nature is love, does.

## VIII

## SEE GOD IN A NEW LIGHT

As one begins to probe more deeply into that infinite room of improvement, the love center within, he is constantly experiencing new feelings of freedom and audacity. Love is always eager to reveal its true nature to the sincere seeker, and he soon finds the courage to probe ever more deeply into the vibrant energy fields he is penetrating. Like the prodigal son in the biblical story, who returned from his session with the pigs in the cornpatch to his father's house and found his father rushing out to meet him, so too the seeker into the nature of love finds love meeting him much more than halfway. As love clears away the smog and the debris of fear and guilt, one begins to experience something of the feeling that must have stirred the enlightened soul who urged that we move into the throne of grace with boldness.

A growing desire to know more and more of the nature of the Creative Spirit makes the seeker willing to depart from conventional patterns of prayer and meditation and move along inspired pathways of his own.

During one of these inner experiences I found a question welling up from deep within me. It was really a question of my soul, and the words that follow are about as close as I can come to framing it and expressing it in readable form: "Who is our Father who art in heaven? Who is the Lord our God? Who is the almighty God, Creator of the universe?"

Immediately the answer began to come, not initially in words, but again as feeling, an inner stirring, a flow of energy. It was as if the whole universe were answering me, opening the forms that constitute it and revealing to me, in it and behind it, fields of light, warm, vibrant energy. It seemed that I was looking into cosmic depths of radiant energy vibrating and flowing into form. As I watched, with instruments of vision I had never used before, it seemed as if the entire universe had become a mouthpiece for the formerly invisible depths into which I could now see and joined in a mighty throbbing song which I can only describe in the words "I AM." As I kept watching and feeling and being delighted by what was taking place, I felt wave after wave of love and joy and gratitude sweep over and in and through my whole being. What I was observing and participating in was so incredibly beautiful, so whole (holy), so incredibly glorious and overwhelming, that my immediate response was an irresistible surge of love from deep within my being. For a moment at least, I loved the whole universe and its Creator because I had caught a relatively uncluttered glimpse of the true nature of being. Feelings of love and praise and thanksgiving welled up within me. I was almost stunned by the beauty of the experience, and the powerful energy current flowing through me lifted my whole being to such a high vibration rate that it was almost unbearable.

I have talked with others who have had similar experiences, and I know that to many others it will undoubtedly seem to be a wildly imaginative tale. But to me, it has been and is a continuing experience in reality. How far it will lead and what direction it will eventually go I do not know, but this is not a matter of concern to me. I am willing to let it unfold as it will.

During another inner experience I asked the shining, radiant presence penetrating the universe: "Almighty Creator, what are you?"

Again I felt that tremendous surge throughout the entire universe, the opening of every form, the vision of the light and radiant energy fields, and then an answer began to form as a feeling, as a growing realization and as a knowing. Again, to put it into words, the answer would be the following: "I am the universal Creative Spirit of love, life, light, and joy. Be still and know that I am."

The immediate response in me was another deep surge of love, rejoicing, and gratitude. There was nothing I could have done to stop that response. It was spontaneous, deep, and powerful. I had caught at least a partial glimpse of the true nature of the Creator, and nothing could stop love from flowing through me to it.

In addition, I began to have a new understanding and feeling for these scriptural revelations: "In the beginning God," "God is Spirit and those who worship God must worship him in spirit and in truth." These experiences that I am attempting to share with you in words are, of course, not just momentary flashes of insight; they are continuing activities that have occurred over a lifetime. They have not been initiated by me, consciously for the most part; rather, they have obviously (to me, at least) been taking place at subconscious or unconscious levels of being, and then, when they are strong enough and mature enough, they come up into my conscious awareness. It has given me a new understanding of this statement of Jesus Christ: "Of myself I do nothing, the Father abiding in me does His works." It is the activity of the universal Creative Spirit of love, life, light, and laughter that is on the job constantly doing its work of awakening and unfolding whoever and whatever it is that I am.

In talking with many others and in reading some of the great scriptures of the world, I realize that I am becoming conscious of the creative process that is constantly going on in all mankind, regardless of the state in which individual members of humanity seem to be. Regardless of the turmoil and confusion, the rise and fall of civilizations, and even the appearance and disappearance of whole universes, the creative process that has produced man and will continue to unfold him goes on. The Infinite love that is the author and sustainer of the whole operation, is not hampered by condemnation, hate, or vengeance. It keeps no record of sin or wrong. It is unimpressed by man's sense of virtue or evil. It continues the creative process in man, sending its rain on the just and unjust, shining its sun on the "good" and the "bad." It constantly pours love, life, light, and laughter into the consciousness of the whole human race, knowing that eventually every soul will be awakened to it, healed by it, freed by it, saved by it, brought into full flower by it. The Creator and the Creation are one. In the great spiritual awakening that is being accelerated in humanity right now, that oneness, that unity, will become ever clearer.

As I observe and experience the activity of the nature of God, the Creative Spirit, I am filled with a wonderful feeling of awe and wonder, of interest and delight, of reverence and worship, of adventure and growth, of praise and thanksgiving. If I were to put that wonderful feeling into one word, it would have to be (yes, you knew it!): love! Or to put it another way: "I love God, the universal Creative Spirit of love, life, light, and laughter with all my heart, with all my soul, with all my mind, and with all my strength." I can readily see that my love is still not very strong, very constant—but under the constant impulse of the universal love, it must grow. I have not reached any final destination and I have yet to meet anyone who feels that he has, but perhaps in a wonderful sense we are on the way, the way of love, which is itself the destination. We are caught up in the eternal process of creation, finding individual expression in each one of us, and the continuing activity of the nature of God in the universe keeps us in love with it.

See God in a new light, the light of your own awakening consciousness. See the Creative Spirit of the universe in the light of love. You need not settle for a secondhand experience of God. Trust the validity of your own experience, your own revelation, your own realization. The universal Creative Spirit is infinite, and it reveals its nature in a unique way to each one. As the creative process of love continues its unfoldment in you, and as you, you will find confirmation of what is happening in the past, present, and future experience of many others—and eventually in all humanity.

Above all, do not be discouraged. Do not compare yourself with others. Do not feel that you are greater or lesser than anyone else. The revelation of the nature of the Creator finds unique expression and experience in and through you. Rejoice in the revelations that are brought to your attention through the experience and the sharing of others, but do not feel bound to or by them. There are elements of the lowest and the highest in all of us. There are insights and states of ignorance in all of us. Our discoveries, our experiences, our realization, and our sharing on the pathway of love have one thing in common—they are equally different. Love the Almighty Creator of the universe, the universal Creative Spirit of love, life, light, and laughter in your own unique and unduplicatable way. See God in the light of your own awakening selfhood. The experience taking place in you is essential to the creative plan of the Infinite. Know this and rejoice!

# IX

# THE WILL OF GOD

As you continue to love, to contemplate, to experience the universal Creative Spirit of love, life, light, and laughter, the realization will dawn in you that this Creative Spirit has a will, a plan, a desire. The will of the Creative Spirit is self-expression, or individualization. The will of the Creator, and therefore the activity of the Creator, is always to give the infinite nature of good in, to, and through its creation. The Creator is always pouring the energy currents of love, life, light, and joy into the universe created to receive, experience, and express them. As your awareness, understanding, and working knowledge of the will of God grows and unfolds, you will find yourself loving the Creative Spirit of love, life, light, and laughter more deeply and completely and powerfully than ever before. Your love affair with God will be an unfolding process within rather than an activity you are attempting to force upon yourself from following outer rules and regulations, good as they may be.

You might frame the experience that is going on inside you in words like the following:

*The will of God for the universe is always an ever-greater experience and expression of the vibrant love, life, light, and laughter that are the nature of the infinite Creative Spirit.*

On the other hand, don't feel that you have to put these inner currents of energy and action into words. Just let them unfold and grow in your consciousness, and you will discover that love is being perfected or expanded in you. In the growth process which is love at work within, you'll discover the truth of the revelation that "love casts out fear." Then these words will be more than just an inspiring statement. They will be the description of a creative, freeing process that is already taking place within you. If you have felt some apprehension or concern about the effect of the will of God in you and your world, it will be dissolved and wiped out of your consciousness and you will begin to realize that the infinite will of the Creator is the most potent element in your maturity and freedom. You will be eager to surrender yourself and your world to the will of the Infinite Spirit of love, life, light, and joy.

Perhaps you would like to take a few moments now to turn to the creative source of all good with words like the following: *O Infinite Spirit of love, life, light, and laughter, what is your will for me and my world?*

The responding flow of creative energy may well knock you off the foundations of limitation from which you have viewed yourself and your world. You may catch at least a momentary glimpse of the love, life, light, and joy prepared for you and held in trust until your consciousness is grown and unfolded so that it can perceive and receive them. You will experience the will of God as a powerful current of energy that co-ordinates and directs the love, life, light, and joy of the universal Creative Spirit into dynamic self-expression as you! It is not an abstract theory that is to be analyzed or discussed or argued about. It is rather the irresistible urge and desire of the universal Creator for individual expression. It is the activity of infinite love wooing, inspiring, drawing, and prodding its sons and daughters out of the ruts of limitation, fear, and ignorance. It is love awakening its children to the paradise that is within and around them, not by imposing outer rules and regulations or herding them into some distant heaven by trying to scare the hell out of them. The kingdom we seek is not an outer destination or place. It is rather the inner potential of man and the universe, which is love itself.

As you practice surrendering joyously to the will of the infinite Creative Spirit of love, life, light, and laughter, you will begin to realize, understand, and experience more completely the truth embodied in the observation of Jesus Christ that the kingdom of God comes not with observation, for it is within you, and you will know with an unshakable faith that this kingdom of God within is made up of the attributes of love, life, light, and joy that are expressing their creative and adventurous energy through you. You will know and have confirmed through actual experience the truth of the revelations that have come through enlightened souls down the ages. You will know and feel and be experiencing the truth that you live, move, and have your being in fields of cosmic energy which we attempt to describe through words like love, life, light, and joy. You will realize that you are at least beginning to share the experience of the one who urged us to lift our vision and to look to the fields that are ripe and ready for harvest right now, or the one who realized that "in Him we live and move and have our being." And of course you will be entering into the revelation, joy, and enthusiasm of the One who taught us to pray, "Thy will be done on earth as it is in heaven."

Practice surrendering joyously to the will of the Infinite Spirit of love, life, light, and laughter, and you will be lifted to higher and more creative and adventurous paths of thought, feeling, and self-expression. The will of the Infinite Spirit will become your own growing desire to experience and express more love, life, light, and joy.

# X

# A NEW SELF-ATTITUDE

Just as most of us have unthinkingly accepted the images, concepts, and beliefs about our Creator and our attitudes toward our divine source from secondhand channels (good as they may be) rather than through actual experience, we have also, for the most part, accepted our own self-image and our attitude toward it from sources other than the actual experience of the reality within us. We are so much the product of our religious, educational, and social background and training that we do not know who we are or what we are. We are so often conditioned or programmed into tight little patterns of thought, feeling, vision, and action that we express only an infinitesimal part of our potential. We often go through life, or most of it, with an uneasy feeling of being "off base," and only on rare occasions, often in times of crisis and emergency, do we catch a glimpse of our real self. At such times we may rise to heights of thought, feeling, and performance that astound us and our circle of family and friends. After such an experience, however, we usually return to the conventional modes of daily experience. Now that our experience in love is beginning to dissolve our old states of fear and guilt, we can begin to take a new look at ourself, to see ourself in a new light.

The experience that we have shared in the earlier sections of this book will continue to grow into a new attitude toward all creation, and, since we are a part of creation, a new attitude toward ourself. It is quite likely that within you, by this time, a

## A NEW SELF-ATTITUDE

new attitude toward yourself is unfolding, and this attitude might be described in words like the following:

*I feel a healthy, dynamic, creative attitude toward myself growing within me. I rejoice in this attitude and I give thanks for it.*

Take the time to enter the room for improvement, the center of love within you, and let this new and healthier attitude toward yourself grow in that inner climate in which there is no condemnation or criticism or self-depreciation or fear or guilt. As you become more deeply aware of the universal Creative Spirit of love, life, light, and laughter, let your natural response of love flow into expression. Then bring that omnipresent Spirit into a dynamic, vibrant focus within your being by asking the universal Spirit, that is, the Creator of all, questions like the following:

"Who is the Lord, *my God,* whom I am to love with all my heart, with all my soul, with all my mind, and with all my strength?"

Then just remain silent, expectant, grateful, and the answer will come. It may come as a deepening silence, as a surge of warm, vibrant, living energy, as a feeling of a radiant, powerful presence within.

But of this you can be sure: An answer will come. If you persist in the practice, it will come even in a realization that can be expressed in words—the words in which the Creative Spirit always expresses itself: "I AM." It will come in such a powerful, glorious way that you will begin to understand what must have happened to the enlightened soul who gave us these words: "Be still and know that I am God." He was listening to the voice of his inner presence, the Lord his God, when this realization came to him. You will understand many other revelations that have come to us in the words of Scripture, insights that tell us there is an inner power greater than our own. There is a light that shines forever in the darkness of our ignorance, superstition, and unwillingness to believe. There is a true self in the midst of legions of our secondary selves, and when we address ourselves to it, it will reveal its presence and power and activity.

As you listen in awe and growing wonder, in delight and gratitude—or, to sum it up more briefly, as you listen in love—the Lord your God will continue to dialogue with you. If you have a sense of humor through which the answer can come, it is quite possible that your question, "Who is the Lord my God?" may be answered something like this: "I thought you'd never ask. I am the Lord your God, the individualized presence of the Almighty One operating in you, through you, and as you. I am the true self, the image of God in you that you have overlooked, ignored, or have been unwilling to believe really existed."

It is unlikely, at least in initial stages, that your dialogue with your Lord will be extensive. What I am sharing with you is not something that happened all at once; it has grown out of a continuous dialogue, or conversation, with the inner reality. Your dialogue may take quite another vein, because the experience of each one is unique and original, even though it will undoubtedly have elements that will enable you to identify what is going on not only in yourself but in many other awakening souls throughout the universe. There are times, as perhaps you have already experienced, when the inner presence speaks spontaneously, awakening you out of sleep or coming into your awareness right in the midst of other activities, constantly making itself known more fully, dynamically, and creatively. If you come across the testimonies of others who either have had or are having similar experiences, you will recognize what is going on in them and you will rejoice with them, as you can be certain they are rejoicing with you. You may wish to deepen and expand the dialogue by asking questions like the following: "Who is my real self? Who am I? Who is the Christ in me, my hope of glory? Who is the Father who dwells in me?"

I find that invariably the same inner presence answers all these questions, and I know that the answers come from one true source. We are, for the most part, beginners in this type of inner dialogue, and as we continue in it, the identity and reality of our inner spirit grows stronger and stronger. I observe this not

## A NEW SELF-ATTITUDE

only from my own experience, but through similar experiences which others are constantly sharing with me.

Another exercise which has evoked a joyous and thrilling response in me is one that came in answer to the following inner action I took. Again, try to see through the words into the action they describe, and if you are so moved, then enter into it yourself: "Will my real self stand up on its feet so that I will know beyond a shadow of a doubt that it hears and responds to me?"

As I waited in expectant love, I could feel a shuffling within the inventory of selves that make up my consciousness, and I could begin to feel, and even inwardly to see, a light-filled selfhood emerging. Its power, its depth, its beauty, and its glory are beyond anything I can describe in words and beyond anything I can accept completely in my present state of consciousness, but as I watched and felt what was taking place inside, I was filled with that same sense of awe and wonder, of joy and delight, of praise and gratitude, that welled up in me when I first felt as an actual experience the universal Creative Spirit of love, life, light, and laughter. I find that the natural response of the so-called human elements of my being is to love this inner self, to revere it, to worship it, to enjoy it, to praise it, to be grateful to and for it. I know the same kind of experience will take place in you as you discover the reality and the power of that divine self, your true being. You will readily agree, I am sure, that one of the best descriptions of its attributes is to be found in the words of Jesus Christ: "The kingdom of God is within." Certainly no king (or queen) in any kingdom could have greater attributes than the love, life, light, and joy that are the nature of the universal Creative Spirit.

Whole libraries of books could be written on the nature of this inner self, but you and I who are experiencing its reality and its power wouldn't have the time to read them. Our unfoldment from this time on is not really a matter of study—although books can be helpful if they spring from the same activity that is moving us. This book can only hint at the scope and the depth and the intensity of the awakening process that is taking place in us.

You may well feel, as you read some of the experiences I have described, that you wish I had expanded a bit in certain directions where you feel led to probe and move. You will readily understand that each of us is on a special pathway, and you may go much further and deeper in certain directions than I do. What I want to do above all else is to encourage you to accelerate and intensify this inner process of discovery, experience, and love so that you can participate more creatively and adventurously in the drama that is taking place in human consciousness now.

Now that you are more conscious than ever of the real self in you, the Lord your God, you will want to turn over more and more of your thoughts and feelings, your actions and reactions, your whole life to it.

You will find it helpful, when you find yourself in situations that tend to draw you back into old patterns and ruts of inner and outer action, to pause a moment and then ask this inner presence, which is becoming so real to you: "Who is willing to be all that I am created to be? Who is willing to express the love and the light and the life and the joy that I am discovering to be my real nature?" You will find quite often that there is a movement deep within you that pushes aside the old self-images and patterns that have held you in bondage to release a powerful current of energy, enabling you to stand up on your inner feet and say in effect, "I AM!"

Certainly some of the elements and experiences of seeing yourself in a new light could be expressed in words like the following:

*I see myself in a new light, the growing light of truth. In this intensifying light I see that I am, in reality, a self-expression, or image, of the universal Creative Spirit of love, life, light, and laughter. I feel the stirring and the emerging of a new selfhood, a self that is no longer quite so bound to old patterns of thought, feeling, and behavior. I love that true self of mine, the Lord my God, with all my heart and soul and mind and strength. It is a natural thing for me to do. In the new light of love in which I see*

## A NEW SELF-ATTITUDE

*myself, old fears and prefabricated states of limitation are dissolving and being washed away.*

George Washington Carver pointed out that anything will yield up its secret if you love it enough. He applied the principle to the peanut, and multimillion-dollar industries evolved from the discoveries revealed through his love. The Lord your God, your real self, is much more than any peanut, and it will yield up its secrets of power and creative energy as you love it. I am sure that within you is the growing realization that you are, in the act of loving your true self, preparing yourself to love your neighbor. Only to the degree that you accept and love yourself can you love your neighbor. That's the way things are in the kingdom of love, that kingdom whose dimensions and energies you are now discovering. It is being activated in you.

You are in the process of getting acquainted with the reality of your inner being, your true self. You will discover that it will respond when you call upon it, and the response is often startling, creative, and adventurous. This true self within us, this God-being that we are discovering, has creative energies and methods at its disposal that our old selfhood feared or did not even know existed.

You will begin to accept and to realize that you are the self-expression of the universal Creative Spirit of love, life, light, and laughter. You will, from actual experience, begin to understand what it is to be the "image of God." You will begin to know and to have confirmed by the revelation of Jesus that the Father, or source within, is greater than you or anything that you have ever dreamed or conceived before. You will realize from what is taking place within you that you are indeed going through a process that is aptly called "a new birth." You are changing your self-orientation, your foundation for living, from outer elements of your being to the inner reality, and this means that you are seeing yourself in a new light, a light that is getting brighter all the time, a light in which you see not only the universal Creative Spirit at work in the universe, but also acknowledge and accept the activity of that Infinite Spirit of love within your being. I am sure the following words from the *Gospel of Thomas* will find an answering chord deep in your soul and spirit, because of what is taking place there:

"Jesus said: If those who lead you say to you: 'See, the Kingdom is in heaven,' then the birds of the heaven will precede you. If they say to you: 'It is in the sea,' then the fish will precede you. But the Kingdom is within you and it is without you. If you (will) know yourselves, then you will be known and you will know that you are the sons of the Living Father. But if you do not know yourselves, then you are in poverty and you are poverty."

You are discovering the Kingdom of Love within, and you are daily becoming richer through your discovery!

# XI

# WAKE UP, EVERYBODY!

After a lecture one evening in London, an enthusiastic young man came up to me and said, "I realized as you were speaking, Sig, that we have to wake up to the fact that we are asleep!" Most of us have been asleep at the switch of our own infinite potentiality. We have failed to realize the tremendous energies and talents that lie slumbering at the inner depths of being. Often in our conventional and habitual patterns of living, we may think we are alive, but we are merely skating around on the surface of life, settling unthinkingly for energies, relationships, and experiences that represent only a fraction of our capacity. We are created to experience and express the infinite power of love, life, light, and laughter, but we rarely take the time to awaken ourselves to the creative and powerful energies that are always available for expression through us. This is particularly true of the fantastic energy of love—the nature of the Creative Spirit within us.

As Teilhard de Chardin puts it so beautifully: "Someday after we have mastered the winds, the waves, the tides and gravity, we will harness for God the energies of Love—and then for the second time in the history of the world, man will have discovered fire."

Through the experiences we are now sharing we will discover the fire of love in and for ourselves. As we take the time and awaken ourselves to it, we will discover that we live and move and have our being in an ocean of love. We are completely surrounded, embedded in, and permeated by fields of cosmic energy (love). These fields are potent, active, vibrant, and the only reason we have missed them is that we have been too preoccupied with the surface of life. Dr. Andrews told me that what we ordinarily think of as the "real" part of life is only the skin, or thin surface, on the world of reality, which is a universe of throbbing, living, vital energies. It is in this deep inner realm that our scientists are finding the truth of the universe, and it is in this deep inner realm within ourselves that we must probe to discover and experience the wonderful truth of ourselves. While a second-hand experience of love is better than no experience at all, it is not good enough for you and me.

By this time you are no doubt discovering through actual experience that "the kingdom of God (love) is within you"—and your major activity is to discover its "righteousness," or the way it operates, and the creative energies it reveals and releases through you. You are realizing, again through actual experience, that there are "fields that are ripe unto harvest already," and that you can begin to reap a harvest that is already sown, not by you but by the Creator. You are tapping hitherto unsuspected energy fields within your reach because your being has its roots in them. These fields are so real that our scientists are beginning to detect them through laboratory research methods. While scientists may label them electromagnetic force fields or use some other scientific designations, they are talking about the same creative energy sources that were discovered by enlightened souls ages ago. As you become more aware of what is taking place at the deep, more subtle areas of being, you will find that the energies that flow from these fields focus, or individualize, into a powerful creative current of energy that is constantly pouring into and through you. This focused, or individualized, current of creative energy is uniquely your own. It has your name on it, your infinite nature in it. This current of creative energy is just as unlimited as the infinite fields of energy from which it arises. You are its product, its image, its self-expression. Whatever it is that you are to be in the unfathomable reaches of eternity that lie before you, it is already contained within this current that "knows its way" to your true selfhood. It is the source of all that you have ever been, are now, and ever will be—the clean, pure stream of being (the Father within), which has never forsaken you through the long ages of your soul unfoldment, regardless of how often you have ignored it, suppressed it, or distorted it through fear, guilt, or inertia. Now you are ready to accept it, surrender to it, and let it unfold you into a new selfhood—a rebirth in love, life, light, and laughter.

You are reaching a high point in your spiritual unfoldment, and as the powerful, creative, adventurous current of love, life, light, and laughter expands its operation in you, through you, and as you, miracles will take place. You will discover (again through actual experience) why Jesus said that the one who accepts his revelation will find that it becomes a spring of living water within, welling up into eternal life. (The great scriptures of the world contain the story of your soul—its bondage and fear, guilt and limitation, and then its awakening in love, and its unfoldment and eternal glory in life, light, and laughter.)

Love is not a lesson to be learned so much as it is an energy to be discovered, accepted, experienced, and expressed. It is a current of creative energy that is present in every individual, no matter how thoroughly he has disguised it and hidden it from himself and others. Loving is an inside job. It is an activity that has its roots in the invisible side of being. Love is the ultimate discovery, the final step which all probers into the nature of the soul agree is necessary before we can be truly free. It is not an easy step, but it is a joyous one because love finally awakens us to all that we really are. Love never "pulls any punches"—so neither will I. Love is the nature of the Creator and therefore of creation. Your real nature and my real nature is love. Love is the "imprisoned splendor," the "mystery that has been hidden for generations," "the image of God" in us—and we will never find any permanent peace, joy, or fulfillment until we are love in creative, dynamic, adventurous self-expression. Love is what you are all about. It is what I'm all about, and it's what this book is all about—so let's move more deeply into the thrilling adventure of love.

## HOW TO LOVE YOUR NEIGHBOR

Right now there is within us a current of creative energy. This current is the activity of the universal Creative Spirit of love, life, light, and laughter individualized in and seeking ever-greater expression through each human being. This current in each person is the creative current of love, life, light, and laughter, and I am going to refer to it as the "L-current" for the purpose of brevity, power, and effectiveness. This L-current has brought us to our present stage of unfoldment, and it is now our special assignment in the creative process to "stir it into a living flame" through consciously becoming its self-expression. As we move more deeply into the creative adventure of becoming love in action, it will make a new creature of us from the inside out and we will find, again through actual experience, what it is to be "born again."

Right now is a good time to alert your whole being to what is about to take place. Speak to every body in your makeup—your mental body, your emotional body, your psychic body, your physical body, and any other body of which you are aware—and let them know what is going on. The following courses of action, outlined verbally, should get you off to a happy start:

*Wake up, everybody! I am in the process of being reborn in love, and you are in for some fantastic and creative changes as the mighty current of love, life, light, and laughter expands its operation in and through me. Off with the old. On with the new!*

## XII

# STIRRING UP THE L-CURRENT

In stirring up the L-current—the current of love, life, light, and laughter—you will be opening your whole being to the most potent energy in the universe. This L-current will leave nothing in you unchanged. Whatever remains of fear and its unloving brood of guilt, hatred, and condemnation are gloriously and inevitably doomed. Whatever remains of death and its unhealthy family of disease, fatigue, burden, and separation are gloriously and inevitably doomed. Whatever remains of darkness and its somber household of ignorance, superstition, and deceit are gloriously and inevitably doomed. Whatever remains of unhappiness and its gloomy retinue of worry, sadness, and depression are gloriously and inevitably doomed. Remember, you are dealing with the stream of living water that is springing up into eternal life, and every enemy of your soul, even death itself, is to be overcome by love, which is the spirit of your Creator, your real self.

Becoming a new creature in love isn't always easy. It is not instantaneous. It isn't magic, and it isn't theoretical—but it is a joyous experience because from the very beginning we realize that we are on our path to freedom, and even in the midst of changing inner and outer worlds there is a deep and abiding joy that often bubbles up in delightful laughter. We are getting in tune with the joy of the Lord, the music of the spheres, the rhythm and harmony of our own soul, and we will discover (again from actual experience), as did that tough-minded warrior St. Paul, that the upheavals we go through are as nothing compared with the glorious grandeur of the vision we have caught and that has caught us.

We are made of pretty sturdy stuff, you and I. We are the offspring of the Almighty Creator, whose purpose in creating us is so great that universes and civilizations, institutions and religions, are only temporary instruments through which it is achieved. Our concepts, our beliefs, our opinions, our habitual patterns of behavior and living are small sacrifices to make for the love and freedom we seek and that we truly are.

In this age of light we are being called to the greatest adventure in human experience—the activation of the spirit of love in the minds and hearts of men, beginning with ourselves, so that the age-old enemies of humanity—fear, guilt, ignorance, superstition, hatred, war, disease, and death—may be brought to an end. Hold this vision as we move together to stir up the L-current of love, life, light, and laughter. If it seems that we are starting such a gigantic project in a small way, remember that just a few years ago the entire Space Age was just a gleam in the minds and hearts of the few who had caught its vision, and for most of humanity the whole idea was so preposterous that it was a fit subject only for the comic strips. Remember Flash Gordon and Buck Rogers? Now we are outstripping the comic strips. Perhaps the age of love and freedom has not made the comic strips yet, but it is being activated in the minds and hearts of many around the globe. Its emergence is just as predictable as the Space Age ever was, and there are more people walking the inner pathway that leads to the freedom of the human spirit than we may suspect. You who read and I who write have been stirred by the mighty L-current that is springing up into eternal life and freedom in all humanity. About the only choice we have is the attitude in which we move ahead on a path that is unfolding in and through us. So let's agree right now that we have a healthy, dynamic, creative attitude toward the L-current, which is the forerunner of our true self.

One of the most stimulating activities we can enter into before embarking on a new course of action is to ask ourselves some probing questions on the nature of our past experience, make an evaluation of the beliefs and concepts that have motivated us in the past. Following are a few that you may wish to answer in and for yourself: Is it possible that we have completely underestimated the potential, the worth, and the role of man in the creative plan? Have so-called religious authorities (and we who have often blindly followed them) made such a din over sin that we have completely overlooked the presence, availability, and potentiality of the kingdom of love within man? Is it possible that the hereafter, the paradise we supposedly seek, is right here after we wake up to the true nature of man and the incredibly responsive universe in which he lives? Is it possible that you and I have been putting off our own salvation, freedom, and true selfhood when it is with us right now, throbbing, creative, alive? Have we listened too long to those who have operated so-called "toll gates" into a kingdom of heaven in the sky rather than taking the direct route to the incredible kingdom of creative energy within ourselves? Have we surrendered our present and future destiny to outer "authorities," even though the record of authorities in almost every field of human experience has not been exactly brilliant, usually turning out to be mistaken or at least limited concepts with a loud voice attached? Is it not time, if we have not already done so, that you and I stand up on our own spiritual feet and become the disciples of our own soul? Are we not ready to drop the subhuman states of fear, ignorance, guilt, and other forms of limitation to join the awakening humanity of love, life, light, and laughter? I have my own answer to these questions (I feel certain that you do, too), and I cheerfully confess that it comes not from some outer authority but from the authority of the quiet and, to me, delightfully refreshing voice of my inner self.

What I am suggesting in this book is that we join in a pioneering adventure into the power and potential of our spiritual nature. I make no pretense and I have no desire or capacity to serve as an authority for anyone else. I decided long ago that the salvation of humanity is not upon my shoulders, much to my relief and the relief of those human beings with whom I have direct contact, and perhaps to the relief of the Creative Spirit whose work salvation is. If some of my statements seem strong and arbitrary, it is simply that I find I have to be firm with myself in what to me is a new way of thought, feeling, and action. I am suggesting possible courses of action which you are obviously free to reject or explore as you will. I have not reached any final destination. I am not sure there is any final destination except in the sense that a way, a path of unfoldment is, in itself, a destination. I feel that I am dealing with the infinite potential of inner being, and it will take at least eternity to unfold that potential.

In the area of being which humanity is forced to explore these days, there is no entry for the fearful, the procrastinating, the lukewarm spirit. A keen desire, a bold faith, and a vigorous will to act are required. I am reminded of a man I met on a trip to the Rocky Mountains. I don't recall that we ever exchanged names, but he told me something of his life, enough to make me so interested that I asked him what his key to success was. He replied in succinct and pungent slang: "To succeed, you gotta wanta! You gotta believe! You gotta do it!"

Until we really want to experience the mighty L-current, our lack of desire keeps it bottled up at its present rate of flow. In fact, we are well advised to stay out of this activity as long as we can, and then, when the desire becomes irresistible, come in with "both feet." A lukewarm or casual interest in the divine current of creative energy produces meager results and can leave us worse off than before. Of course, we are always free to experiment, and even a little activity in a lukewarm state of mind will soon convince us that, since we are neither "hot nor cold," love does indeed "spew us out of its mouth." When getting a more sumptuous meal for our tummy, getting a better job, driving a bigger car, owning a lovelier home, finding a more attractive or compatible mate, achieving outer success and fortune (important as they are in their own realm) mean more to us than finding, experiencing, and expressing our true nature, then these are our "thing," and we should "do our thing" until it

## STIRRING UP THE L-CURRENT

is done. Inevitably, all lesser projects wear themselves out in us, and we come to the point where necessity, frustration, or boredom stirs up the desire for the highest adventure of our being. Once the desire in us is activated to the point of irresistibility, we move into the next phase—faith.

When we put our faith into the inner L-current of love, life, light, and laughter, it responds immediately and powerfully, according to our faith. If we do not believe in the presence, power, and activity of the L-current, we simply are not using one of the greatest factors in expanding its operation in us, and its flow is only a trickle of what it might be. Here again we have the opportunity to prove to ourselves, through actual experience, that without faith it is impossible to please or experience this inner God power. We are, of course, free to exercise our faith in all lesser things until we have thoroughly demonstrated that they cannot satisfy our deep desire for our true nature—or we can stir up our faith and put it to work in the energy fields of being and the L-current that flows from them in and through us.

The next and equally important phase is doing it, or perhaps more accurately, letting it be done in and through us. If we are unwilling to let changes be made in our present state of mind and heart, in our attitudes and decisions, in the relationships and patterns of our inner and outer world, we are in a wonderful position to prove to ourselves, through actual experience, "that faith without works is dead." In such a state of inertia we might be compared to an old-timer in New England of whom the story is told that he was rocking on his front porch one bright, sunny morning when his longtime friend Ezra came down the street. Ezra said, "Zeke, what's the matter with you this morning? You look like death warmed over. Did your wife kick you out of bed or something?" Zeke replied, "No, I'm just getting old, I guess. Nothing seems worthwhile any more. Nobody cares anything about me. I guess there is nothing left to do but die." Ezra, trying to stir him up a bit, said, "Zeke, don't be like that. Life has something wonderful for you to do!" Zeke rocked along for a while and finally announced his decision, "I ain't a gonna do it!"

## HOW TO LOVE YOUR NEIGHBOR

We can only assume that Zeke rocked along in his limited state until he wound up in the grave he had largely dug for himself. While it may be "hard for an old rake to turn over a new leaf," it can be done if we have the desire, faith, and will to let the mighty L-current do its work in us.

Now, if you feel ready to do so, you can carry these courses of action into that secret place of your inner being where the stream of living water, the mighty L-current, eagerly awaits you. Don't make a big project of it. Do it simply. Simply do it. Be as alone as the circumstances permit. Relax as much as you possibly can. Turn quietly inward and center your attention on the "stream of living water," even if it is only a mental abstraction to you now. Speak to it. Until you have words, thoughts, and feelings of your own with which to activate this current of divine energy, the following may be of help:

*Mighty L-current of love, life, light, and laughter, I want you, I believe in you, I am willing to let you renew my mind and transform my whole being.*

Perhaps your desire, your faith, and your will are so in tune with the experience we are sharing that the response from the mighty L-current is instant and electrifying. Perhaps you have experienced the flow of energy that leaves you breathless, startled, and delighted. But even if nothing much seems to happen, do not be concerned. You are at least in the position to demonstrate that desire, faith, and will the size of a grain of a mustard seed can be developed, expanded, and grown into a current of energy that can activate and sustain a whole new way of life. This is a wonderful time to remember that "laughter is a good medicine." Take yourself joyously. Remember this is not a somber, heavy business. We are involved in a lighthearted, open-minded, happy approach to a new way of life. Even if this simple way seems ridiculous to you, bring to mind the great truth that it is only as a little child that you can enter this inner kingdom of love, life, light, and laughter. Probably most of us are not a little child in love yet. We may be in the embryo stage or just getting pregnant with this new life potential. So take a few minutes, relax, and

## STIRRING UP THE L-CURRENT

laugh a bit before you repeat the experience. You may be trying too hard, and this is not a kingdom that can be taken by force. Even if you decide to drop the whole thing for the time being, do it joyously so that you can return to the project at the right time, in the right frame of mind and heart.

Recall all the truth that you know about yourself, from actual experience preferably. Remember that a new way of life, a new state of consciousness, begins like a seed that is planted in the ground, which produces first a blade, then a stalk, then an ear, and then the full grain in the ear. Remember that this new breakthrough, small as it may seem at the present time, is like yeast in dough, and it leavens the whole thing. Remember, too, that there are rocky and hard places in your consciousness. There are elements in your being that may try to reject new concepts and courses of action. But there are also elements in your being that are constantly seeking the new, the creative, the adventurous way of life. Remember, too, that you are a creature of free choice, and you can use your freedom of choice to continue to move ahead in this new way or try to return to the old. I say "try to return to the old" because, if you have read this far, you have come too far in the new way to return completely to old states of bondage and limitation. If it is your decision, then once again focus—and, incidentally, you might take a look at that word "focus," which can be interpreted to mean "freedom of choice, used spiritually"—focus your desire, your faith, your will, your attention on that stream of creative energy, the L-current, and go ahead as you are inspired and moved to do. You may wish to use the same words as before, or a procedure that will unfold within you, or you may wish to experiment with some suggestions such as the following:

Tell yourself, *I enjoy what I am doing. I enjoy the way the L-current in me responds to my desire, faith, and willingness to grow and be changed. I am utterly delighted by the way the current of love, life, light, and laughter expands its operation in me, through me, and as me.*

Or you may wish to try the procedure of dialoguing with this L-current. Ask it how you can help to expand its activity within you. You may be surprised at the result of such a dialogue. It may speak to you literally in words, or as thoughts and feelings, or as a movement of energy inviting you to accept it, praise it, appreciate it, acknowledge it, surrender to it, affirm it, congratulate it on its power and activity, to just relax and let it take over. Then do what you are moved and inspired to do.

As your dialogue with the mighty L-current continues, you will discover many things through your own experience. You will find why the poet urges that we converse with the Creator—because He listens and responds. You will have a personal insight into what must have taken place in the mind and heart of the one who realized that the inner voice spoke, saying: "Be still and know that I am God." You will understand how another unfolding soul discovered that "the joy of the Lord is your strength." You will discover also that many of the words used in this book are no strangers to you. Even if you do not ordinarily use the words in the context in which they are operating, you will be familiar with the activity that gave rise to them. For example, there will be an activity taking place in your experience that might be described in words like the following:

*I rejoice in my growing ability to stir up the mighty L-current within me.*

*I praise and give thanks to the L-current that fills my whole being with love, life, light, and laughter.*

*I am grateful for the marvelous and miraculous ways in which the L-current is expanding its operation in, through, and as me.*

*I praise the L-current that wipes fear, death, darkness, and gloom out of my mind, heart, and body.*

Or perhaps a prayer, like the one that came to me during one of the upheavals that the L-current frequently precipitates in its expanding operation, may strike a responsive chord in you:

*Father, tickle the hell out of me! Infinite Creative Spirit of love, life, light, and laughter turn up the L-current in me until its vibrations dissolve, dislodge, and drop out of my being all the hellish states of my mind and heart that have kept me from being less than you created me to be.*

## STIRRING UP THE L-CURRENT

Gradually you will realize that there are deep and subtle changes taking place in you. Gradually, although often spectacularly, surges of power will flow through all of your systems of self-expression, your heart, soul, mind, and body. You will realize, as others before you have, that the function of this L-current is always to bring forth a new creation. You will begin to see and feel that you are literally becoming a new creature, oftentimes seemingly against the waning influence of your old concepts, beliefs, and attitudes. You will realize, again from actual experience, that it is not really you who are doing the work but, as another pioneer in this field put it, "the Father abiding within doeth the works." Your part lies in accepting, surrendering to, and letting the action initiated by your desire, faith, and willingness take over. Now that you have given the L-current of love, life, light, and laughter the "go ahead," the stream of living water is welling up into eternal life within you.

Something new is being born in you, a new creature is being brought forth, and in that burgeoning newness you will see yourself in a new light.

## XIII

## SEE YOURSELF IN A NEW LIGHT

*See yourself in a new light.* Even these words have a lifting, freeing influence, don't they? The reason for this is that the awakening elements in your being sense even greater things to come. The L-current within rejoices in its new freedom of operation, its new creature of self-expression. You, too, are beginning to rejoice in the realization that never again can you return completely to old states of fear, guilt, darkness, and frustration. You will no longer fit comfortably into the old limited ruts of operation, even though you may have occasional lapses, or what appear to be lapses, in the expanding activity of the L-current within you. You will sense the stirring of a new state of selfhood. You will realize that a miracle of love, life, light, and laughter is taking place within you and you are no longer what you were a few short years, months, days, hours, minutes, events ago.

You will begin to see yourself in a new light, not so much by a conscious effort or struggle on your part, but as part of an element in the progressive unfolding of the L-current in you, through you, and as you. It will dawn in you that you are the product of the Creative Spirit of love, life, light, and laughter expressing its selfhood as you. You will understand more fully than ever before the meaning, activity, and power of the creative process described by the two words "I AM." You will have a deepening insight into the revelation, shared by many, that the name, nature, and activity of the Creative Spirit is always "I AM"—individualization, embodiment, self-expression.

You are discovering that words are quite inadequate when it comes to describing the deep inner changes that are taking place,

## SEE YOURSELF IN A NEW LIGHT

but the following will at least hint at what is unfolding in and as you:

*I see myself in a new light. In this new light I see (and feel) that I am the individualization, embodiment, and self-expression of love, life, light, and laughter, according to my desire, faith, and willingness to let them operate in me, through me, and as me.*

Or in a slightly different way:

*I see myself in a new light. I see (and feel) that I am the L-current—I individualize it, I embody it, I give it self-expression.*

I know you realize that these are not just affirmative statements that you are repeating to try to make them so. They are rather words describing, in an inadequate but joyous way, a process that is taking place. In this new and intensifying way in which you see yourself, you will realize that many of the old concepts and limiting self-images that you have given power to bind you no longer exist. In the new light they are no longer binding. But they were certainly stifling your real potential while they held sway. I think it was the humorist Josh Billings who said something to the effect that it is not so much what we don't know that hurts us as what we do know that just ain't so! In the past we have all known plenty of things about ourselves that "just ain't so," and they hurt, didn't they?

One of the startling realizations that comes as we see ourselves in the new light generated by the L-current at work in us, is that we are not just poor flesh-and-blood mortals struggling to get back into the good graces of our Creator. In this rapidly increasing light we can see that we are in reality spiritual beings being awakened by a mighty current of love, life, light, and laughter to the truth of our own nature and potential. Each one of us is a self-expression of the infinite Creative Spirit, partaking of that infinity and sharing it with our world according to our desire, faith, and willingness to do so.

In the growing light that the L-current generates in your being you will undoubtedly, like many others, gladly reject the old concept of being conceived in sin and born in inequity. The commandment is that we are to honor our father and mother—not accuse them of sin and inequity. You will have fresh insight into the revelation of the one who declared that we have one Father, and that is the Almighty God, or Creative Spirit. From the spiritual viewpoint of truth, you are conceived in love, animated by life, illuminated by light, and strengthened by joy. As you come into the recognition and realization of your true selfhood, even from a so-called human viewpoint, you will realize that you are conceived in and born in love at whatever degree of understanding your human parents had. At this joyous realization you may breathe a prayer of thanksgiving to the infinite Creative Spirit of love, life, light, and laughter for having brought this light into your conscious awareness and understanding. What is taking place in you might be described in words like the following:

*I see myself in a new light. I see (and feel) that love is the source, cause, and sustainer of my being. I rejoice in the new sense of freedom that the L-current is unfolding in me.*

The intensifying light in your being may become so bright that you will enter into the revelation that came to the Psalmist, who saw that all men are gods, sons of the Most High, and share in the revelation of the One who reaffirmed this earlier insight, and added to it the observation that they are called gods to whom the word of God, or truth, is delivered. The L-current of love, life, light, and laughter delivers the word of truth into your consciousness, and if you are ready and willing to accept the delivery, you will see yourself in a new light as an awakening god—an offspring of the Almighty Creator. If you wish to test your own inner state, watch your reaction as you repeat the following statement:

*I see myself in a new light. I see (and feel) myself as an awakening god—an offspring of the Almighty Creator.*

If you are like most of us who have been thoroughly programmed and conditioned into a false and limited state of selfhood, this statement may seem a bit strong. So you may wish to rephrase the same idea in milder terms such as the following:

## SEE YOURSELF IN A NEW LIGHT

*I see myself in a new light. I see (and feel) that I am a spiritual being—an offspring of the infinite Creative Spirit of love, life, light, and laughter.* Or, in the new light, you will certainly see that you are a self-expression of the creative L-current, which is your source of all things, urging you and moving you to the acceptance of a higher image of yourself. One word picture that I particularly like is the following, because it seems to incorporate all the elements of the L-current in an active state:

*I see myself in a new light. I see (and feel) that I am love in action, a life-giving spirit, the light of the world, joy at work.*

Or: *I see (and feel) that I am a loving, life-giving, radiant, joyous spirit.*

Any of these expanding images will provide increased room for the L-current to operate. And, of course, by this time you will have many new revelations of your own.

One of the most interesting and helpful forms of meditation that I know is simply to enter consciously into the presence of love, become quiet, and let what wants to happen happen. It reminds me of an experience I shared with my wife at beautiful Emerald Lake in the Canadian Rockies. We had just finished a very busy lecture trip, and the deep silence and beauty of this lovely spot invited us to empty ourselves of all sense of fatigue, rush, and strain and let ourselves be refreshed and renewed by the love and life we felt so deeply there. After a few moments in such a lovely atmosphere one can feel the L-current most clearly, and at such moments of deep meditation I find it inspiring to simply let my inner self realize its selfhood. To describe the process, in admittedly inadequate words, would bring forth a statement somewhat like the following:

*I see myself in a new light, the light of love and life. In that light I see (and feel) that I am—I know that I am—I know who I am—I know what I am doing.*

This inner process is not an attempt to force something, or even to do something; rather, it is letting all the elements present focus themselves into a realization of selfhood, of individuality, of embodiment. This is a self-realization that embodies both universal and individual aspects of selfhood. It is simply a knowing of the self in God—in love, in life, in light, in laughter and joy. It is a knowing of the truth, the truth that sets us free from all lesser concepts of selfhood.

Some may ask if this type of inner action leads to inflating the balloon of the ego to self-conceit. On the contrary, it leads to true self-humility. There is nothing quite like catching even a brief glimpse of our real self on the one hand, and checking what we have done with it on the other, to make us feel truly humble.

I now ask you to review in your mind and heart what you have learned about love through actual experience. You have found that love keeps no record of past mistakes or the false images you have held of yourself. It accepts you as you are, where you are, without judgment or condemnation, encourages you to catch and hold as high a vision of yourself as you are willing and able to do, brings as much light as possible into your consciousness, so that you may see your real self more clearly. Then love immediately releases the L-current into that vision to make it real and expand it beyond anything you have conceived. This is one of the most important revelations and realizations that can come to you as you learn to love your neighbor as yourself.

As the "seeing-yourself-in-a-new-light" experience continues to deepen and expand, you will find a subtle and marvelous change taking place in your thoughts and feelings. This change might be described in words like the following:

*I see myself in a new light. I see (and feel) myself to be a loving, life-giving, radiant, joyous spirit, and I am beginning to think and feel like one.*

Or: *I see (and feel) myself to be an offspring of the Infinite, and I enjoy expressing myself mentally and emotionally like one.*

Do not be too tied to the words I am suggesting. If they fit what is happening in you, fine. Use them. If not, use your own words, thoughts, and feelings to describe to yourself the process that is taking place in you as you see yourself in a new light. The important thing is that you learn to trust your own revela-

## SEE YOURSELF IN A NEW LIGHT

tion, have faith in your own growing consciousness of the L-current, and accept the worth and validity of your own experience. What is taking place in you, while it may be similar to what others experience, is completely unique—more unique than your fingerprints, your voiceprint, or your thoughtprint. You are a divine original—treat yourself like one. No one else can do it for you!

## XIV

## BE YOURSELF

It is one thing to find yourself—to catch even a fleeting glimpse of your potential as the self-expression of love, life, light, and laughter. It is quite another assignment to be yourself in the tug and pull, the busy demands of daily living. But this is what love requires and inspires us to do. There is a delightful story, told in many versions, about a man who died and suddenly found himself at the gates of heaven. St. Peter, or whoever was operating the gates at that particular moment, didn't ask, "Why weren't you like Moses or Elijah or John or Peter or Paul or even like Jesus?" He merely asked, "Why weren't you yourself?"

If love were ever to ask us a question as we enter its gates in our own inner being, it might well be: "Why aren't you yourself?" That is a good question to be asked and to answer. Why don't you answer that question now in the spirit of love, life, light, and laughter? If you answer honestly (and that is another of love's requirements, self-honesty), you will find new insights into the fantastic assignment you and your neighbor have as human beings. You will realize that being human is the greatest assignment love has given any of its creatures. You will begin to understand the distinction between heaven and earth, and at the same time, their inseparableness. You will quickly gain a new realization and respect for the prayer, "Thy will be done in earth, as it is in heaven." You will understand more clearly than ever before that heaven is not a place or destination toward which you are headed. It is rather your spiritual self-potential which is to be brought into expression in your relationships and activities right here on this very earthy earth. You will find that if you love yourself enough to be true to yourself, you cannot, as has been pointed out, be false or unloving to anyone else.

You are, as I pointed out in the last chapter, a divine original. In all the starry reaches of creation there is no other creature quite like you. You are designed to give unique and unduplicatable self-expression to the inexhaustible L-current of love, life, light, and laughter. You are free to use that current of divine creative energy as you choose, but of course you are responsible for your choice. Self-responsibility is another of the requirements of love.

You must find your self in heaven. You must be your self in earth! You must find your self, your true self, in the only place where it is to be found, in the inner kingdom of love, life, light, and laughter. Here you will find "the mystery that has been hidden for generations"—Christ, or love, in you—not only your hope of glory, but your guarantee of wholeness and freedom. Love is your true self, the spirit that you are.

As you see yourself in the new light, the light of being, your enthusiasm to free yourself, to be yourself, may rise so high that you share the feelings described in the following words:

*Sometimes I throb with laughter and tingle with glee as I contemplate the delightful, incredible, joyous project of being me.*

Of course the inevitable prod from love comes: "Now you have found yourself in me, go out and be yourself in the world. You are now to be about my business, the business of love, the business of being your true self." Your shock at this startling bit of news might be akin to what the prodigal son must have felt after he returned to his father's house only to learn that he was to go back into the world once again, this time about his father's business, not his own; or the chagrin that the disciples of Jesus undoubtedly felt when he told them he would not pray to get them out of the world but only that they might be kept free from the clutches of the evil one.

And who is the "evil one"? Ah, you know him only too well, don't you? He is your old self, the fearful one, and therefore the evil one, whose name is legion. He has been identified in such descriptive terms as "Satan," "the Devil," "the Adversary," "the Great Deceiver," "the Old Snake in the Grass," "the Tempter," who will use every trick in his voluminous bag to try to draw you away from your new assignment in love, being true to yourself. For a time, at least, along the new way you are traveling to be yourself, he'll empty his "bag of tricks" into your path. He may use the pressure of conformity, the anger of rebellion, the threat of ostracism, the promise of power and comfort, the glitter of wealth and affluence, or as a last resort, the doleful promise of condemnation and eternal hellfire. Oh, he is a wily old skunk, this evil one; but seeing yourself in a new light, you will also see him in a new light. You will see him for what he is: a bundle of fear, a windbag, a trickster, a counterfeit, loudly laying claim to power that is not his—and to the awakening spirit of love, life, light, and laughter that you are becoming, you will see him as a "has been." In greater measure than you yet realize, you are no longer afraid of him, and to the degree that you no longer fear him, he has lost his power over, and in, you. I do not suggest that your way will always be easy or that there will not be times when you will be tempted by or even succumb to his wiles —but your victory is sure in the mighty L-current that is expanding its operation in you, through you, and as you. You have the energies that will overcome the evil one and wipe out the fearful remnants of your old self. Love always wipes out fear. Life always overcomes death. Light forever dissolves darkness, and laughter and joy always bring sorrow to an end. Perhaps you will even see this old Devil fall from his throne in your consciousness as a flash of light and realize that for you the Devil is dead. You may share some of the thoughts and feelings outlined in the following realization:

### SATANIC DEATH

The Devil is dead!
He died last night
and right
after the news

of his passing came out
legions of believers—
both friend and foe—
rose with loud and frantic shout
to insist it could not be so.
Leaders of mighty institutions,
grown fat and rich
through battle with or for him,
now search desperately for means
to revive his satanic majesty—
sure the work of centuries must crumble
as the news travels from mind to mind
and men no longer find
a ready scapegoat for immaturity!
But—the Devil is dead—
for him there is no resurrection,
no power connection
strong enough to bring him back!
Why and how did he die?
Some say the "Liar and Father of lies"
saw the handwriting on the wall of time—
describing his inevitable demise,
and he was wise
enough to give up the ghost
more quickly than most
of his supporters.
Others feel he tired of wickedness and deceit
and on the brink of final defeat—
repented of his sins
and won over by the love of God—
laid aside the old "snake in the grass" mask
and turned his skills to good endeavor.
Yet others declare he was but
the darkness in man,
and the light is now too bright
in many minds
for him to live.

In any event,
for all with eyes to see
and ears to hear,
the message is clear—
The Devil is dead!

This mighty L-current is the cross that Jesus advised his followers to take up and to deny or cross out the old false sense of self in order to enter, experience, and share true selfhood. It is also the power used by Moses to lift up the snake of false belief and limitation in the wilderness so that the light might shine for the children of Israel. It is also the current in you that "knows its way" to your true selfhood, and now that it has your pretty much undivided attention, will fill your whole being with light and dissolve what remains of the darkness and fear of your former self.

There are those who reach this point of awareness of their true self and who try to remain in what seems to be a paradise of beauty and perfection, resisting the move back into what they term the world of matter and illusion. They may protest that they want to live in a world of reality. Both heaven and earth are realms of reality; in fact, earth is the realm where we test our consciousness of reality and practice it. Others may return to earth bemoaning their fate at being called to live again in such an ugly place, beseeching the Father to set them free so that they may have their "reward in heaven." The reward that heaven has to offer is another chance to live a more inspired, love-filled, freedom-oriented life in the practice fields of earth. Others—and I am sure this includes you—return to earth gladly, knowing that while they are "in this world" they are no longer "of it." They have "meat to eat" that their old world knew little of. They are drawing their love, their life, their light, and their laughter from an inner current beyond the reach of their former self. When "the prince of this world" comes—when old habits of fear attempt to reassert themselves—he finds less and less of a reaction in them. They are no longer so "taken in" by his promises or moved by his threats.

You will find, I am sure, that the ability to love and to live without fear does not come in a single bound, a single day, or a single experience. There will be "ups and downs," "ins and outs," in your unfoldment, just as there are in all those who are traveling the path to true selfhood. Behind every new creature and species that have appeared or will appear in creation, there are countless eons of preparation, incredible amounts of energy, and no doubt considerable "growing pains." The butterfly emerges from the cocoon in a relatively short time, but you can be certain that a great many things have gone on in that cocoon before it opens and the beautiful creature takes flight. You are the product of the creative genius of the universe. Eons of time, rivers of love, life, and light have brought you to the point where you now are. Do not be discouraged if you are not, instantaneously, on earth what you see yourself to be in heaven. The creature of love, life, light, and laughter whose outline you have glimpsed in heaven has some unfolding to do in earth. While the Bible speaks of the "twinkling of an eye" in our awakening and freedom from bondage, you can be certain that that eye had been attentive to the inner light for a long while before it twinkled. Of one thing we can be sure, though: Right now, this day, is the acceptable time, and our present earthly surroundings the acceptable place, for us to start to move into the great adventure of being true to ourselves.

If you still have a few moments' time before actual involvement in a relationship, a job, or some other activity, you may wish to review briefly what has been happening to you. Perhaps you will realize that you are not really what your world thinks and assumes you are. You are not what your family or your friends think you are. You are not what your enemies think you are. You are not even what you thought you were. You are, to yourself at least, a new creature, and in many ways a surprising and startling one. You are discovering and uncovering a delightful ability to be honest with yourself. You may look over the whole broad outline of your life and at specific relationships and situations in which you are involved. As you look at them honestly and also—since you are a creature of love, life, light, and laughter—without fear or condemnation, you may find that the reason for your involvement is not what you have assumed it to be. You may well discover that you are involved in rich, vital, mutually profitable relationships and situations. In others you are still involved, even though you have outgrown them (which usually means that others involved have outgrown them, too), and you remain because of a sense of obligation or duty, a desire to please, the fear of hurting someone if you make a change, the bondage of habit, the fear of starting a new way of life, and many other reasons. In almost every unhappy or unproductive relationship or situation, you will find evidence of conformity to some kind of pressure, or rebellion in some degree against it. The happy, creative, and productive relationships and situations pose no immediate problem. In some measure you are being true to yourself in them.

Now let's take a further look in love at what you might admit are problem areas in your life. If you have detected the elements of conformity and rebellion in yourself concerning these areas, you are also realizing that at their root is that old devil fear, who is rapidly losing influence in your attitudes and feelings. You can see that fear leaves us only two routes—conformity or rebellion. Your growing awareness of yourself as a creature of love, life, light, and laughter opens up a new way of action that is neither conformity nor rebellion, but the activity of being true to yourself. You can, then, rejoice in this growing realization even though you do not understand it completely yet. You realize that you need no longer conform to or rebel against tired old patterns of living, but that you can become what I like to think of as a Spiritual Independent, by being true to yourself—your inner spirit of love, life, light, and laughter. Just the thought of this possibility brings such a feeling of freedom that new and creative courses of action will unfold from within you, and you will know deep within that many of the problem situations are being solved. In addition to this, you will probably perceive that many of the seemingly rich and profitable relationships and situations in which you are involved are not nearly what they might be or will be, as you move with growing joy, confidence, and enthusiasm into being yourself.

You are now at a wonderful, crucial, and adventurous point in your adventure of learning to love your neighbor as yourself. You have come into a new understanding and appreciation of the first two steps in this creative process, loving God and loving yourself—being true to God, the spirit of love, life, light, and laughter, and being true to yourself, the individualized expression of the universal Creative Spirit. You understand that it is impossible to love God, to be true to the universal Creative Spirit, without loving and being true to yourself. Now you are discovering that you cannot love, and be true to, yourself without exerting an immediate and profound influence upon your neighbors—the people in your life. I realize that you have other "neighbors"—your pets, your home, your environment—but this book is primarily involved with people neighbors because, as you learn to love them as you love yourself, your whole universe, its creatures and its environment, will benefit too.

We will explore some more of the elements of this creative adventure of loving your neighbor as yourself. I know that you are writing this book as surely as I am. We are sharing this experience and finding the ideas and course of action outlined here a confirmation of what has taken place, is taking place, or will take place in you and me. In many ways you are far ahead of anything that appears in this book, because love is such a potent energy it can never be confined to a book, but finds its release and growth and development in our minds and hearts and lives.

## XV

## LOVING YOUR NEIGHBOR

Just as in loving yourself, there are two phases in loving your neighbor. It is relatively easy to love your neighbor in heaven—that state of awareness where you can see, feel, and realize that your neighbor, even as you, must be a self-expression of the universal Creative Spirit of love, life, light, and laughter. In this ideal state, you cannot resist the feeling of love, delight, joy, and appreciation that rises up in you naturally as you contemplate the wonderful spirit that you are and that your neighbor is, in truth. It is good that we can see this reality of our neighbor, this altogether lovable spirit, this ideal self-expression, this child of the Father of us all. Without this inner picture and the enthusiasm and incentive it generates in us, we probably would not even undertake the much more difficult assignment of loving our neighbor in the earth. (If you wonder why I use the expression "in the earth" rather than "on the earth," it is simply because we do not really live on the earth, we live in it—for example, the atmosphere, the clouds, are just as much a part of the earth as the trees, the mountains, and the streams. Realizing that we live "in the earth" gives us a deeper sense of involvement in what goes on in this beautiful globe.) Loving our neighbor in spirit is one thing, learning to love our neighbor in the flesh is quite another. An astute and sensitive observer has pointed out that it would be easy to love our neighbor if it weren't for people!

So since love put us right here on the earth to learn its lesson through practical experience, we might just as well get on with the assignment.

To get back to the point in our last chapter where we came to the realization that we could not love ourself, be true to our real self on this earthly plane, without immediately involving other people, you have no doubt learned a great deal through the exercise you have been following. You have discovered that in so-called problem areas, relationships, and situations, where you feel forced to conform or rebel, you have been reacting negatively in your feelings with some elements of fear or its train of irritation, resentment, burden, procrastination, or frustration involved. From your experience with your true self of love, life, light, and laughter, it is readily apparent that these negative reactions are not part of your true, or higher, self. *Fear* (and its whole stable of unattractive offspring) *is always a reaction.* Fear is a thought or feeling of self-concern based on insecurity, stemming from the belief that something that someone has done, is doing, might do, or might not do, will take something away from us. Love, on the other hand, *is always an action* based on the secure knowing that it has nothing to lose because it possesses nothing and yet is all.

Love is like light. In fact, light is one of its manifestations. Scientists have discovered that light is complete in and of itself. It is not something existing in something else. It is not dependent on anything else. It doesn't draw its nature from anything else. It is light, and it shines because it is light. It acts out of its own nature and is not concerned because it shines on a very dark night or in a dark room. Jesus used the sun to illustrate the nature of love. He said it shines on the just and on the unjust and pointed out that the rain falls on the deserving and on the undeserving alike. A delightful story is told about how the sun and the lesser ones in the heavens got together to discuss the darkness on the earth. Several had gone down and reported tremendous darkness in many areas. The sun said, "I will go down to the earth and see for myself," and then returned to report to the others that it had not been able to find a single dark spot on the earth. The sun shines because it is the sun, and love loves because it is love. So, too, it is with the one who is learning to be true to his real self. He loves because he is love. He lives because he is life. He shines because he is light, and he laughs because he is joy. He acts not in conformity or rebellion but because he is true to himself—a creature of love, life, light, and laughter. He is a Spiritual Independent, neither deflated nor inflated by the opinions, actions, or postures of others, real or imaginary. He is learning to be true to the integrity, or nature, of his own inner being. By now you realize through actual experience that the reactionary or fearful self must decrease, and the self of creative action, the self of love, must increase.

Let us examine a bit more deeply what we are doing when we react negatively in a relationship with another. First of all, we are being very unloving to ourselves by being untrue to our real self, and this becomes more painful and destructive all the time. Then, we are making a very unloving and unlovely gift to our neighbor by giving him the power to make us react in a negative and destructive manner.

Is there any way to be true to yourself in a situation like this, to let your real self gain the initiative, move from negative reaction to positive and creative action? Of course there is. To say it is impossible is the equivalent of saying it is impossible to turn on the light in a dark room. Simply stop reacting, and then let your self of love take over. If you are within verbal reach of your neighbor so that he can hear you, say something, depending on the circumstances and what you are guided to do. Say something loving, lovely, or romantic; something lively, vibrant, or creative; something light, radiant, or inventive; something joyous, humorous, or laughable—anything to get the L-current flowing again. If nothing else, start to laugh—at your own immaturity; the humor of the situation, or just because you are mature enough to laugh. At least it will give your neighbor an opportunity to ask, "What's so funny?" It will start the conversation and communication lines going again. It is better that your neighbor think you are some kind of "nut" rather than discover your momentary immaturity and—so often to his surprise, dismay, and unhappiness—that you have been acting in a fearful, resentful, or unloving way. Love operates in earth as well as in heaven, and we who are becoming its self-expression do, too.

Once we get the hang of it, we will be so busy with the activity of love that we will have less and less time to give to the reactionary activity of fear. We will become so sure of our new selfhood that, in a very real sense, we can forget it. We will move from self-concern to self-expression. We will find that we can take the spiritual initiative in love in more and more areas, relationships, and situations in our life. We will be loving our neighbor as ourself by being true to ourself in his presence. Certainly we can pay another person no higher compliment and give him no greater gift of love than to be our loving, life-giving, radiant, joyous self in his presence. If we do it often enough, sincerely enough, and happily enough, it may even inspire him to go and do likewise.

Let's look once again at what we are discovering. *Fear reacts, love acts.* Love commits itself wholeheartedly to life, acting spontaneously and continuously out of the fullness of its own nature. Fear, on the other hand, always reacts from a sense of lack, either apparent or anticipated. The reaction of fear may come so quickly that it seems almost an action, because we have done it so often and established a habit of it. Fear inhibits, suppresses, distorts, and finally brings to at least a temporary halt the flow of the L-current. Love activates, stimulates, and increases the flow, even to the proportions described as eternal life.

Any situation or relationship in which fear and its elements are allowed to operate without interruption becomes stagnant, destructive, and deadly. Love in action in any situation or relationship keeps it alive, stimulating, flowing.

I recall an incident from my early career as a salesman that illustrates this point. I had obtained an appointment with a busy manager of a large firm whose business I wanted to obtain and cultivate. Since I was new in the selling game, I had carefully rehearsed everything I was going to say, and the gentleman in charge was polite enough to listen for a long time. Finally, even my inexperienced salesman's sense told me that things were not going too well. My prospective customer was at the least bored, probably irritated, and even a bit hostile. I pushed even more frantically, and finally he interrupted my sales pitch in an abrupt and rather startling way with these words: "Paulson, why in the ----- should I buy anything from you? For all I know, you won't even be in business a year from now, and if you continue this approach it is absolutely definite you won't be. You have taken nearly an hour of my time—and I'm a busy man, as you can undoubtedly see—to hear all the reasons why I should buy your product, your company, and you. You have demonstrated perfectly that you know nothing about me, my business, the products I handle, the needs I have—all you are interested in is getting an order." Startled and a bit shocked at the accuracy of his observation, I started to retort, but suddenly I caught the warm twinkle of interest and friendship in his eye, so I said, "You are right. What do you suggest?" He replied, with a big grin, "I suggest you take the next hour just going around my store talking to some of my employees, looking over my merchandise, and especially going into the basement where I do most of my business." I had an interesting time meeting his associates and coworkers and looking over his merchandise and getting a feel for the way he conducted business. I went back upstairs again and my hoped-for customer was tied up with another salesman. He waved and grinned and said, "I am too busy to see you again right now, Sig. Come back next week and let me know what you learned." I called on this busy man at least ten or twelve times before he gave me a first order, but by that time the order was secondary. We had established a delightful and mutually rewarding friendship, and doing business with each other over a number of years was really a fringe benefit because he had had the interest, good humor, and what I would call a deep sense of love, to break his own chain of negative reactions and initiate a new activity. If he had thrown me out on my ear, as I so richly and ignorantly deserved, I was much too sensitive to ever have entered his place of business again. In the years since that initial contact we have often laughed over how our rich and rewarding friendship, and what we both agreed was a mutually profitable business relationship, were established.

Laughter, good humor, are such a vital and important part of our life, and they seem to be an indispensable part of the L-current and experience. Sometimes laughter itself seems to be a door opener in rich and creative relationships. I have met people with whom the first exchange was laughter. Something about each other, the fact that we really had no designs on each other and no desire to manipulate or exploit each other, established such an instantaneous sense of love and freedom that we just had to laugh about it. After all, the Creative Spirit must have quite a delightful sense of humor, or it would never have brought forth humanity in the first place. If God were a person, which He is not ("God is Spirit"—Jesus), He would have to have a couple of angels around His throne just to pick Him up and replace Him after He laughed Himself into near collapse over some of our human antics. (Perhaps in this day of "women's lib," I should say He/She. You have heard the delightful discovery made by one who probed into the nature of God and reported that "She is black!") I am sure that in addition to being a technicolor God, our Creator has all the elements of the L-current; in fact, the Creative Spirit must be the sense of humor that bubbles up in us every once in a while.

I had a delightful experience during a seminar when a woman came up and thanked me for making clear to her why she and her grandson could just look at each other and laugh themselves into near hysterics. She said that the rest of the family seemed to think they were a bit insane. Now she realized that they just loved each other and felt so free with each other that laughter was the best means of instantaneous and deep communication.

I am deeply grateful for the wonderful sense of humor that my family and friends have displayed in putting up with some of the antics I have gone through in the project of finding and being myself. I give thanks for that delightful sense of humor, which may be called upon for even greater service in the future as the joyous, challenging project of selfhood unfolds.

Laughter seems to be a good note on which to continue what we are doing. Won't you join in?

## XVI

# SPIRITUAL INDEPENDENTS LEAGUE

Deep down inside me I knew this would happen. The tempo of our experience is picking up. I feel the need to go even more deeply into the awakening process of selfhood, so I call to your attention an idea and course of action revealed through the teachings of Jesus, the Christ, and St. Paul. This is really accepting and claiming the new birth process as our own. You will recall that Jesus said it was impossible to enter into the kingdom without a new birth in spirit, which I interpret as meaning that we have to move from the old flesh-and-blood status with its fearful reactions and anticipations to the full realization that we are eternal, indestructible spirit, the offspring and image of God, the universal Creative Spirit. St. Paul sounds the same note in one of his letters to the Corinthians when he says that the first man became a living soul, but the second man becomes a life-giving spirit. He further states that the first man is of the earth, earthy, and that he carries all the fears, hangups, and inhibitions of the earthly man, but that eventually the second man, who is the Lord from heaven, comes along, and then as we have borne the image or patterns of the earthly, we begin to put on the heavenly. In the context of the ideas and experiences we are sharing, we might say that our first sense of selfhood is pretty well filled with elements of fear and reaction—the second one, which we are now entering together, brings us to the realization that we are spiritual, or we might say love in action. Regardless of our limited understanding of what we are to be, we are to start where we are in consciousness and let that new creature, which is a life-giving spirit, unfold in us. In our fearful, reactionary state we have believed ourselves to be the victims of all kinds of conditions, circumstances, situations, relationships, people, problems. In our ignorant state we have usually put the blame for our difficulties on something outside ourselves, an inscrutable fate, a wily devil, the will of God, or life itself. In our awakening state of selfhood, we are at least beginning to accept self-responsibility, not so much in a negative or guilt-producing way, but as a step toward our own freedom. As we do this and begin to move in the directions that are revealed in and through us, we are finding that new elements of our selfhood keep popping up.

I don't know what a "life-giving spirit" is. Do you? I am sure that the worm in the cocoon would find it impossible to describe the butterfly, that beautiful winged creature it is to become; but it probably feels some vague stirrings in its being, which it cannot comprehend, even before the cocoon pops open. We have probably been stirred from time to time by elements of our own self-potential, either from within or through assistance from others—so the promise of what we are to be is undoubtedly making itself known in various ways.

I am reminded of a delightful story shared with us by Samuel Uba Oti, who is now president of the Unity movement in Nigeria. He and the then president of the Unity movement, A. Njoku, who was killed during the Biafran War, visited us at Unity Village. I don't recall all the facts of the story, so I will exercise considerable license in repeating it. My dad used to say, "Never let the facts spoil a good story." So I'll accept his insight and admonition in this instance. With all due apologies to my good friend Sam, here is the story as it has grown in me:

It seems that a farmer and his two sons were out walking, when they came across an eagle's nest with an egg in it. One son said, "Dad, shall we smash this egg?" The other son said, "No, Dad, let's take it home and put it under one of our hens and see what happens." So that is what they did. In due course, the egg hatched and a young eagle bounced out and became a member of the chicken flock, eating chicken feed, sunning himself, and grabbing an occasional clawful of dirt to throw over himself, as all conventional, good little chickens are expected to do. Kocklebert, the head rooster, and Cacklebert, the mother hen, and all the little Eggleberts were at first somewhat concerned about the strange bedfellow and his unchickenlike appearance; but he, having no mirror to check himself out, just assumed that he was one of the chickens.

One day a couple of eagles high in the sky, probably practicing power dives with some enterprising seagull, chanced to spy the young eagle, who had now become known as Jack the Rooster, in the chicken yard. Startled, the one who made the discovery shouted to the other, "Hey, isn't that one of us down there in that chicken yard?" The other took a quick look and then said, "Wow! We better get down there and check that thing out."

As the shadows of the descending eagles hit the chicken yard, all the flock, led by Kocklebert, dashed frantically for cover. Jack the Rooster looked up, but, perhaps stirred by some as yet unawakened element in his eagle heritage, he looked curiously at the two handsome birds who landed on the fence surrounding the chicken yard. One of the eagles called out to Jack and said, "Hey, buddy, hop up here on the fence for a while, will you, please?" Jack, in obedient chicken style, gave a big hop and landed on the fence. One of his as yet unrecognized brothers said, "What are you doing down here in the chicken yard eating chicken feed and making little round holes in the dust to sun yourself? You're no chicken. You're an eagle. You're one of us." Jack just looked at them curiously, but he didn't say anything. The other one said, "What's your name?" Jack replied, "I'm Jack the Rooster." The reply came immediately, "No, you're Jack the Eagle. Can't you get it through your thick head that you are one of us and not just a chicken. Take a look at your wings. They are magnificent. They're just like ours. What do you do with them?" Jack reared up proudly and said, "I wave them up and down like this on those mornings when Kocklebert, the head rooster, lets me take his place in greeting the rising sun." And then a bit ruefully, "I'm not a very good crower, but Kocklebert says with a few more lessons I should be able to get by." Laughter shook the two visiting eagles so powerfully that they almost fell off the fence. Then they looked disgustedly at each other and soared off into the blue sky. Jack looked after them with a strange kind of longing in his heart, then he shook his head and hopped back down into the chicken yard, calling his chicken family back to their interrupted daily meal of chicken feed and dust.

The two eagles returned to the fence a number of times, trying in vain to persuade Jack that he really was an eagle. He just wouldn't believe it; but each time he remained on the fence a bit longer after the persistent friends had flown away, pondering and trying to understand what they had told him. One day the two determined eagles hit upon a master stroke. They persuaded a beautiful girl eagle to come with them. After listening to her and looking at her for a while, Jack began to experience some decidedly unchickenlike thoughts and feelings. Jack was still not completely convinced, but after the trio had flown away he remained longer than usual on his fence perch until they were but specks to his awakening eagle eyes. Then suddenly, with a happy laugh, he spread his eagle wings and soared out after them.

After this strange occurrence, Kocklebert and Cacklebert and all the little Eggleberts talked it over. Said Kocklebert, "It's for the best. He always was too big for his britches." Added Cacklebert, "Yes I know, but he was such a fine young fellow. He tried so hard to be a chicken, and he was such an interesting addition to our little family." All the obedient little Eggleberts agreed with both viewpoints.

All of which illustrates in fable form that if you can get an eagle young enough, put him in a chicken atmosphere, feed him chicken feed, teach him to scratch the dust and sun himself in it, he will begin to think, feel, and act like a chicken, even becoming chickenhearted in the process. It often takes a great deal of persuasion to get him to realize what he is. Ironically, Kocklebert and Cacklebert and all the little Eggleberts were eagles too, but they had been chickens for so long they even looked the part.

## SPIRITUAL INDEPENDENTS LEAGUE

You have probably heard or read of the community of two-legged creatures that had a "freak" born into it. This strange creature had two funny-looking lumps on his shoulders. Naturally, he became the object of much ridicule, teasing, and downright torment on the part of his conventional fellows. One day, racing to keep ahead of his tormenters, he became so frightened that he suddenly spread his wings and flew out of their reach.

Sometimes it takes persuasion, sometimes it takes pressure, before we are moved to try our unsuspected and unused spiritual talents and energies. Possibly some of the persuaders and the problems in our lives are not so much negative or destructive as they are invitations to spread our spiritual wings and do a little soaring under our own power.

Perhaps you will be willing at least to jump up on the fence with me for a bit to take a look at some of the persuaders. You might be interested in checking out their names. If you look down the fence, you will see that there is a man-god by the name of Jesus, the Christ. There are Moses and Elijah and Elisha, Paul and John, Mohammed, Buddha, Gandhi, Ralph (Emerson), Walt (Whitman), Teilhard (de Chardin), Kahlil (Gibran), George (Washington Carver), Martin (Luther King), Richard (Bach), Charles (Fillmore), Ernest (Holmes), Emmet (Fox), Joel (Goldsmith), and—not to leave out some of the early "women's libbers"—Ruth, Mary (the mother of Jesus), Mary (Magdalene), Mary (Baker Eddy), Helen (Keller), Myrtle (Fillmore), Nona (Brooks), and many others. The list is imposing. You and I are on the fence, at least temporarily, and now we can decide whether we will hop off the fence or fly off.

Jesus pointed out to those in the chicken yards of his day that they have always had prophets and persuaders but that they treated them pretty roughly, stoning them, torturing them, killing them. Gratefully, in this age of relative and growing enlightenment, we no longer treat the persuaders quite so roughly, but for the most part we seem to be successfully ignoring the revelations.

I don't know very much about what kind of creature this life-giving spirit is, but I am willing to start where I am and find out. How about you? I like the sound of the words "a life-giving spirit" and the vibrations and currents of energy they stir within me. I also like the sound of the statement "I am a life-giving spirit" and what it does to, in, and for me. And you? Are you willing to take a last look at the chicken feed and dust that the old man of earth has been eating and say, "It is finished! I am through that portion of my experience. I don't know exactly what I am saying or letting myself in for, but I do declare, 'I am a life-giving spirit.'"

I also want to extend to you an invitation to be a member of an organization. I have never had too much interest in organizations, but this is rather an unusual one. It has no rules or regulations. It doesn't even have a head, but it does have a heart of love, and that's enough to insure its operation. It does have a name, at least tentatively: "Spiritual Independents League." It will be made up of those who are accepting their spiritual independence, declaring that they are "a life-giving spirit," in the long, deep, silent reaches of their souls.

The idea for this activity comes through a beautiful friend on the East Coast, who says she got it from something I once said. It has always surprised me how quickly someone will pick up an idea that I have voiced and put it to work in effective action. Ideas are universal, and just because they come through us doesn't mean they belong to us, unless we really accept them and put them to work in our lives. I remember Joel Goldsmith's telling me that he really had to study the material that came through him before he could accept the full import of it. It is interesting to ponder a bit on what would have happened in our lives if we had told ourselves that we are a life-giving spirit as often as we have recited our statute of limitations, or if we had remembered that we are love in action as often as we had reacted to our fears. But, then, there is little use in wasting our energy, wondering. Let us instead use it to put the following ideas to work within us:

*Love in action is the life-giving spirit that I am. I am a life-giving spirit, and I rejoice in the mighty L-current that has brought me to the point where I can accept it. I am one eagle*

## SPIRITUAL INDEPENDENTS LEAGUE

*of spirit who is taking off from the chicken coop of limitation to try his own wings.*

Speaking of wings, I am sure you will enjoy the following ideas from Kahlil Gibran. "God has given you a spirit with wings on which to soar into the spacious firmament of Love and Freedom. Is it not pitiful then that you cut your wings with your own hands and suffer your soul to crawl like an insect upon the earth?" I am deeply and eternally grateful to the lovely person who sent me this selection. I have not lived up to it too well, but every once in a while when I feel in a particularly "wormy" condition I read it, and I feel my wings growing again.

Speaking of clipped wings and fables, here is another story you may enjoy.

There was an angel who looked down upon the earth and decided he wanted to be born into the human family so that he could have a living experience on this lovely globe. His friends warned him it would be tough going, but he persisted and picked out a wealthy family where he felt he would have the best advantages. In due course he was born, and the attending physician and nurses were aghast to find that here was a baby with a pair of wings growing out of his shoulders and neatly folded on his back. Realizing this must be some kind of mutation or freak, they hurried to the father and told him of the surprise waiting for him in the delivery room. He said excitedly, "Isn't there something you can do about this? This is horrible. My son will be some kind of freak and wind up in a zoo or museum." "Of course," the doctor assured him, "if we have your permission, we can easily remove the wings surgically. There will be only minor scars to show that they were there at all." The father agreed, so the doctor, after checking with the local board of the medical association, and the head of the ministerial association, to get the blessing of the clergy on the whole operation, removed the wings. The new father and mother heaved a sigh of relief, and since they could afford it, promised handsome rewards if nothing was ever said of what transpired. Everything went along fine until the boy reached his teens, when one day he became so curious about the scars on his shoulders that he cornered his mother and father and insisted that they tell him what was the cause of them. Under intense pressure they told him the whole story. His first question was, "Where are the wings?" The mother said, "Oh, of course, we had them burned. We didn't want anything like that around." The boy said, surprised, "Oh, why didn't you save them with that lock of hair from my first haircut?" Then brightening a bit, "It's okay, folks, I understand and I forgive you. After all, a fellow cannot afford to be too different from the rest of the gang, can he?"

Even in a fable we have a tough time breaking through the blanket of limitation that is placed over us.

Now read this, and it isn't a fable. For the most part, we take our children fresh from the golden meadows of love, life, light, and laughter, put them through our religious, educational, and social systems, firmly clipping their spiritual, mental, and emotional wings in the process, in order that they might become one of the gang in the chicken yard of conformity and limitation. I have often thought that the major problem with children is that they become like their parents and other adults too quickly, rather than becoming the winged, life-giving spirit that the Creator designed each one to be.

It is wonderful to realize, too, that though our wings may have been clipped by well-meaning teachers, preachers, parents, and friends, we are always free to become silent but active members of the Spiritual Independents League and let our wings heal and regrow themselves. All we need do, as Newton Dillaway says in his book *Consent,* is consent to the current that knows its way, and it will do the rest. As someone has said, "Decisions, decisions, decisions, always decisions." We have one now. Is it back to the chicken coop or up into the sky? The following idea in words may give you a boost:

*I am a life-giving spirit, and I reach decisions like one!*

## XVII

## GIRD YOURSELF WITH LOVE

You have been seeing and feeling, inwardly and outwardly, the results of seeing yourself in a new light. We are now ready to move into the freeing activity of seeing our neighbor in a new light, but before we move more deeply into that process, I would like to suggest that you take a moment to feel the sense of joy that is beginning to operate in your mind and heart. This is a joyous enterprise in which we are engaged. The freedom that comes from laying aside old habits, thoughts, feelings, and attitudes is sheer joy, the joy of love and life and light.

No one can be attuned to the activity of love or plugged into its cosmic energy field without becoming a lively, radiant, joyous person. The somber and overly serious way of living is coming to an end. Even if you have been a fairly happy and radiant person, the more deeply you move into the golden meadows of love, the more turned on you become and the more alive, radiant, and joyous you are.

A friend was talking to a young man who had become pretty deeply involved in taking drugs. He tried to explain that there was no need to take stimulants, intoxicants, or drugs to get turned on and to feel the depth and joy of life. After listening for a time, the young fellow said, "Oh, but you are different. You are stoned in the natch!" When we are really turned on from within and the L-current is free to operate in us, through us, and as us, we begin to glow with a light and joy that cannot come by any other means.

What we are doing as we share together the experiences outlined in this book is becoming aware of and making ourselves receptive to energies already present with, in, and around us. In the presence of plenty, abundance, and overabundance, we are so often weak, starved, and poor because we have been made unwilling, through fear or conditioning, to accept what we really are. No matter where we begin our probe into the true nature of man, if we are persistent enough, faithful enough, and willing enough, to penetrate the mirage of limitation that surrounds us, we are completely awestruck by our discoveries. Dr. Andrews said that if we could find some way to release the atomic energy in the human body and convert it into electricity, each one could rent himself out to a great city and supply the energy needs of such a metropolis indefinitely. What a way to solve the energy crises that the world faces right now! Other scientists have studied the human brain and discovered that it contains billions of cells, each one able to store millions of items of knowledge. Others have discovered that every cell in the body is an intelligent and complex universe, every bit as wonderful as the body itself. Others acknowledge that every time we accept a new idea completely, the entire chemistry of the body and its performance change. Still other researchers have learned that every atom in the body is replaced every few months, and from a certain viewpoint there is no reason why the human body cannot be eternal, because it is a self-renewing mechanism, or organism. Is it possible that the reason the body seems to stay pretty much in the same old rut is that we don't accept enough new ideas to change its chemistry? Perhaps there is a constant flow of pure atoms and cells from the invisible energy fields in which we live and move and have our being, but our states of mind, our beliefs, our attitudes radiate such a powerful and consistent atmosphere that the body seems to be either relatively unchanged or to go downhill. That's something to ponder, isn't it?

When we get into the realm of mind and spirit, even the wonder of the body is completely surpassed. It is claimed that geniuses use only a fraction of their potential. Some of the most enlightened researchers of all time have checked into the spiritual, mental, emotional, and physical potentialities of humanity and declared that man is made in the image of God or that he is a god, an offspring of the Most High; or that he is a little lower than the angels right now, but has the capacity to rise even higher; or that the kingdom of God is within him and that he is the light of the world; or that the mystery that has been hidden so effectively through generations of ignorance is in reality the Christ of God in man; or, in the context we are using and experiencing, that while man has yet a long way to go to put the finishing touches on himself, he has the capacity to become a life-giving spirit. Fortunately, no one knows exactly what that means, so it is pretty difficult for anyone to come up with a formula that will produce perfect results and that he can copyright and merchandise. Ultimately, every man must come to the realization that he is a creature of infinite potential and that he is going to have to accept and express that potential. He can sit around marking time, waiting for saviors, individuals, and institutions to work magic in him, but eventually he will discover that the only thing he gains from sitting on his own potential is a bunion on his sitter. Jesus told his disciples that if he did not pull out of their immediate presence and leave them on their own, the spirit would not and could not come to them. He told them he would not pray them out of this world, he would only pray that they manage to stay out of the clutches of the evil one, which means the old fearful self with its habits of inertia, procrastination, alibis, and self-depreciation.

There is no way to love our neighbor until and unless we love ourself. There is only one self in the universe, just as there is only one God, one love, one life, one light, one breath. This self, which is the Christ of being, the Divine Ego, is the universal life-giving spirit. It is the Word which was with God in the beginning and which was God. In this divine word is the life and the light and the joy of man. Every person is the expression of that divine self, an expression that is fearful or loving according to his own understanding and experience of it.

Each one is responsible for loving himself—or the divine self within him. This is a responsibility he cannot pass on to anyone else, to any other organization or institution. The late President

Harry S Truman had a sign on his desk which said, "The buck stops here," meaning that eventually responsibility ends up with the President. You are the president of your own nation of thought and feeling. The responsibility for accepting yourself, for loving yourself, for freeing yourself is your own. If it were not, you would be only a robot—perhaps a very intelligent and wonderful robot, but you could never really be free unless you had the responsibility for doing that.

I am reminded of a letter I received from a woman who had responded to some of the ideas in my book *Your Power to Be*. She said that her grandson had been spending the summer with her, and one day she realized that there was something wrong with him. He just wasn't his cheerful, radiant self. He seemed to be depressed. He was wandering around the house without even seeming to realize what he was doing. She tried everything she could to reach him, but to no avail. He was obviously upset and concerned about something. Then one day he came running in from the yard, his face aglow, his eyes sparkling, a big smile on his face, and in a happy voice he said, "Hey, Granny, guess what?" Delighted she said, "What?" His joyous reply was, "I changed my own mind myself!" And isn't this true of all of us? We must ultimately come to the point where we reach our own decision, make up our own mind, change it. Even if we are determined to find our way through the opinions of others, or organizations, or institutions, we eventually have to decide which opinion we will accept—and no matter how good it is it will be a secondhand opinion, which keeps us at least one step from our own selfhood.

Somewhere along the rocky road to self-realization we will discover that there is an eye in us that is ready to twinkle. We will suddenly realize that we are on the verge of becoming a new creature and that usually this is a long-overdue realization. We are willing to begin at least the move from self-preservation, selfishness, and fear to self-acceptance, self-expansion, self-growth, and self-sharing. There is no set time or place for this experience. We may be deep in a meditative mood and in an ornate cathedral, church, or synagogue; we may be in various

## GIRD YOURSELF WITH LOVE

stages of winning the whole world at the cost of our true self; we may be in a flophouse on skid row, a penthouse on luxury avenue, a lake in the Ozarks, or on an island in the Pacific; we may be a saint or sinner to human eyes; we may be on top of the world or seemingly carrying it; we may be running or paralyzed; we may be addicted to drugs, drink, money, or violently preaching against them all; we may be playing any role on the human stage, but the time will inevitably come when we will realize that we are ready to crawl out from under our security blanket of conformity, rebellion, explanations, alibis, and other forms of self-deception, because we will have come face to face with the "hound of heaven," the dynamic, creative, indestructible life-giving spirit which is our true self. We are then confronted with the decision. Are we ready to accept and to love this radiant inner spirit? or do we turn away and continue on the same old merry-go-round for a while longer? If we decide that the old show has gone on long enough, that the time for a change is at hand, we come to ourself, and we can begin to experience a growth and expansion of our true self-potential by loving it. If we hesitate too long, checking out all the authorities who supposedly know better than we do what we are to do, we lose out temporarily and have to start the old cycle of serving "lesser gods." We go through the painful experience of once more sitting on our self-potential and we realize that "on the plains of hesitation bleach the bones of countless millions, who at the very dawn of victory, sat down to wait, and waiting—died" (William Lawrence).

Loving, accepting, and being ourself is a deep, soul-expanding experience. Not only do we have the inner pressures of habit, experience, and fearful attitudes to rise above, we have plenty of outer pressures toward conformity and against accepting ourself as a unique, creative expression of the Infinite. This is a time of bigness in outer things. We have big religions, big labor, big business, big welfare, big society; giant, well-financed, expertly run institutions and organizations tell us what our religion should be and spell out the penalties of nonconformity; others outline what we should believe in almost every field, what we should think, how we should vote, what our duties to ourselves, others, and society are, what we should wear awake or asleep, what we should eat and drink, how we should change the establishment, and even how many of us will die on our highways over certain holidays. Computers threaten to rub out what little individuality we retain by making us statistics, filed away on cards and tapes. But as we grow in love we realize that these outer pressures are in reality the mold in which true individuality and selfhood are to be discovered, accepted, and expressed. Deep in our being, that inner voice is saying, as it did in times of old, "Gird up your loins and be a man" (or in this day of women's freedom, "Hitch up your girdle and be a woman"—on the other hand, there is no reason why a woman's loins shouldn't be girded, too!).

Right in the midst of our present conditions, circumstances, society, environment, there is an inner urge to put on the whole armor of our inner self—the armor of love, life, light, and laughter. We and the rest of the world have demonstrated that we can't fight our way out of limitation, because the fighting is in itself a limitation. We can, however, begin to laugh, and it is surprising then how many of the limitations will drop out of our consciousness and therefore out of our life. I like what Walt Whitman says: "Celebrate yourself." It reminds me also of a sign I saw on a motel on the East Coast a few years ago. It was right in the midst of the initial ecology awakening, and here is what the sign said: "Preserve wildlife—throw a party!" And that's exactly what we should do to preserve and expand our sense of spiritual life—throw a party in our own mind and heart. Celebrate the awakening and the coming forth of our true self. Stand up on our own feet. Stop evading, hiding, running. Rejoice and be glad for the whole package of our selfhood, that inner kingdom which our Creator finds pleasure in giving to us! Take a fresh look at our self-potential as the image, the self-expression of the Infinite Spirit of love, life, light, and laughter. Breathe the breath of the Almighty into that infinite, creative, awakening, life-giving spirit that we truly are. Enter some new rooms in the divine mansion of divine selfhood. Come alive with the mighty L-current of love, life, light, and laughter.

## GIRD YOURSELF WITH LOVE

We need no longer try to fight our way out of our inner and outer establishment. Just let a new creation take place, and it will produce miraculous results. I met a good friend one morning and his eyes were shining. I asked him what pleased him so much and he said, "Something funny happened on the way out of bed this morning. I changed my mind, my thoughts, my feelings, my attitudes, and my whole day changed." If we are tired of the old bed of limitation, we can let something funny, joyous, happy, delightful happen within us and move right out of it.

Right now, perhaps you will wish to join me in throwing an inner party, a celebration of the divine self, the life-giving spirit that we truly are. Make it an inner activity, knowing that this is one love affair that is nobody else's business—at least not right now. Take the following words and the ideas they contain deep into your inner center of love, life, light, and laughter:

*I am a life-giving spirit and I celebrate myself with growing confidence, joy, and enthusiasm.*

Realize that these words are not just an affirmation of something you are trying to establish within yourself; rather, they describe a state of receptivity, a willingness to accept the truth of your own being, a willingness to open yourself completely to the mighty L-current of creative energy. You are letting yourself reveal its true nature in and to you, and that is the occasion for a real celebration.

This desire to be yourself is not of your own doing. The cosmic energies of the universe have been trying to find a more complete and joyous self-expression through you—and through me—and through all humanity. Now we are ready to accept that inner action and let it unfold in its own creative way.

Continue your happy inner celebration with the following course of action:

*I am a life-giving spirit, a self-expression of love, a life distributor, the light of the world, the joy of the Lord—and I love myself, deeply, freely, joyously, without embarrassment or reservation.*

## HOW TO LOVE YOUR NEIGHBOR

Remember that anything will yield its secret if you love it enough. You can apply that wonderful principle to yourself and bring forth a whole new world of being and self-expression. Love is not just a nice little reward with which you pamper yourself. It is the dynamic creative energy that sustains and unfolds the whole universe.

Jesus said that he did what he saw the Father doing. Have you taken the time to observe what the Father, the universal Creative Spirit, is always doing? I did it for a few moments on a canoe trip to Canada, and I discovered that the Father is always loving his universe by filling it with life, light, and joy. We who are made in the image of the Creative Spirit are called upon to do the same thing in ourself and our world. Perhaps you'd like to expand what you are doing by entering the activity described in the following words:

*I continue celebrating myself, loving myself, by giving life to everything I touch mentally, emotionally, and physically.*

Obviously, I could fill another book with these joyous statements of receptivity, but since you are also caught up in this creative, unfolding action of the life-giving spirit that you are, you will find your own. They will bubble up from within you in great bursts of love, life, light, and laughter. Now that you have pulled the cork on your own limitation, your life will become more and more a time and experience of celebration. Congratulate yourself on the mighty work that the Creative Spirit is accomplishing in you now that you have surrendered to it. You may wish to put it into words like these:

*I congratulate myself on being a life-giving spirit, the image of the infinite Creative Spirit.*

Naturally, you will also find that from time to time remnants of your old state will come up for review. You may occasionally catch yourself descending on the escalator of negative thought and feeling. You may even be tempted to succumb to it, but as you become stronger and stronger in your new sense of selfhood you will be able to dismiss it with a thought like this:

## GIRD YOURSELF WITH LOVE

*I am a life-giving spirit and I dispose of these old hangups like one.*

The power of infinite love has you more firmly in its grasp all the time, and it will reveal the ways to cast out the demons of fear, unhappiness, burdens, possessiveness, and ignorance which have plagued you in the past.

You are putting on the whole armor of love, life, light, and laughter, and you are being shown how to deal with and to stay out of the clutches of the evil one, the tired, fearful, old selfhood that is dying out in you.

## XVIII

## SEE YOUR NEIGHBOR IN A NEW LIGHT

In learning to celebrate yourself, to accept yourself, to love yourself, to enjoy, free, and appreciate yourself, you are well on the way to loving your neighbor. You see clearly that you are caught up in a creative process which is love unfolding itself in you, through you, and as you. You can look back into your life experience as far as your consciousness will permit you to see and realize that you have come through many stages of self-unfoldment. Like the prodigal son, you have probably been in the corn patch with the pigs a number of times. You have gone through states of ignorance and confusion, fear, bewilderment, isolation, and separation when you have struck out blindly and violently at your world. You have, no doubt, gone through stages when you attempted to convert and save the world by getting it to accept your own particular concepts and way of life. You have gone through many stages of awakening to your true inner self. You had moments of insight and revelation when everything seemed to be just the way it should be, and then have been thrown back into experiences in which you felt that everything was lost.

Now you are coming into a state of selfhood where a new sense of freedom and strength is being established. You are more stable in your thoughts and feelings. You have caught the vision of a world of creative activity and cosmic energies that make you realize you are much more than you ever dared to dream or suspect. You have felt something of the power of the mighty L-current of creative energy, and you certainly must suspect that there is much more than you have yet uncovered or

## SEE YOUR NEIGHBOR IN A NEW LIGHT

experienced. You are no longer so quick to judge yourself or condemn yourself or to judge others or condemn them. You have a much deeper, gentler, more patient, more creative, healthy, and dynamic attitude toward yourself. You can see that you have not attained perfection, and that you are in no great danger of attaining it in the next breath or two. Also, you are beginning to shed some of your old fears, your old statutes of limitation. You are able to look at some of the events and experiences that would have unbuttoned you emotionally just a few months, or years, or even days ago. You can laugh at them now and also stir up a great deal of mirth at some of the antics you went through, when you were almost completely in the dark as to the reality of your inner being.

All of this growth in your awareness and understanding through actual experience has already worked and will continue to work a subtle change in your attitude toward other people. You will realize that you are not anybody else's judge. You will see that each of us, in a very real sense, travels his own pathway. When he is in the dark, when he is bound by ignorance and superstition and fear, your neighbor will strike out at the handiest target available to him. You will understand this and feel a deepening compassion for him. This is loving your neighbor as yourself.

You're daily experiencing the thrilling energies of love, life, light, and laughter as they expand their operation in your whole being and daily make you a new creature. You are undoubtedly feeling so grateful for what is taking place in you that your prayers are becoming more and more a song of praise and thanksgiving. You have caught a glimpse of the real you, that dynamic spirit of love, life, light, and laughter that is your true nature. Your growing sense of freedom and strength, your growing insight into life, and your growing enthusiasm for the activity taking place in you, through you, and as you, fill you with a deep desire that others may experience this same movement toward selfhood. You want others to know this marvelous freedom, this deep and abiding joy. You will extend this desire, not only to those nearest and dearest to you in the family setup of things, but to all humanity as well. This is loving your neighbor as yourself.

You are daily seeing yourself in a new light. You no longer think of yourself as "just flesh and blood," a poor human being tormented by conditions and situations, circumstances beyond your control, people who don't understand or appreciate you. You are seeing yourself, to some degree at least, as a spiritual being expressing your creative energies of love, life, light, and joy through constructive thought and feeling, words of power and truth, attitudes that are dynamic, creative, and adventurous, work that is challenging and inspiring, relationships that are rich and productive as you release the full power of your creative spirit into them. You realize that you are not nearly as bound as you used to think you were. You are probably beginning to realize joyously and gratefully that if you had been the victim of anything, it was not so much people and circumstance as your own attitudes, thoughts, and feelings and the way you looked at yourself. In the growing feeling that this new perspective brings to you, you will be seeing your neighbor in a new light, the light of truth, the light of his true potential. This is loving your neighbor as yourself. Perhaps you will want to pause occasionally during the day and say to yourself:

*I see myself in a new light. I see my neighbor in a new light. This is loving my neighbor as myself.*

You will realize at this point in your spiritual unfoldment that you are dealing not just in words or statements. You are dealing in attitudes, patterns of thought and feeling, courses of action that are rising more and more from deep within your being. You will realize—and this from actual experience—that you radiate waves and currents of energy into your universe and that your world responds to the radiations you give forth. You will find, again from actual experience, that you live in a responsive universe, that your attitudes are contagious and that they are caught and responded to by everything in your universe, particularly the people in it. You will discover—and this may be a disconcerting discovery at first—that not only does your world

## SEE YOUR NEIGHBOR IN A NEW LIGHT

respond to your attitudes, but you have to look at your world through your attitudes. You may be startled to find that your opinion of another person tells more about you than it does about him. Our opinion of someone else usually turns out to be only a description of our own attitudes toward life, toward ourself, toward people. You will discover—and this becomes an exhilarating experience—that "your enemies are those of your own household." And you will realize that these enemies are not members of your family, circle of friends or acquaintances, people seemingly opposed to you in one way or another, but rather members of your inner household, those attitudes that "people" your mind and heart, those ways of looking at yourself and your neighbor that bind, irritate, and suppress you. This inner awakening may indeed help you to see many of your neighbors in a new light. You may be guided to move some of them from your "enemy" list to your friend list—or at least to your "friendly enemy" list, because you will see that they are serving a friendly purpose, reminding you of some inner areas where growth in love is essential for you. You will find, from actual experience, that in your present as well as in your past, your best friends often turn out to be those whom you have found the most difficult to love. In forcing you to dig down into your spiritual resources to turn on, often in desperation, the mighty L-current of love, life, light, and laughter, these friendly enemies are doing you a much greater favor than others who, through their own weakness or ignorance, leave you undisturbed in upholstered ruts of narrow attitudes and smug limitation. This often disconcerting and even painful realization is one of the facets of learning to love your neighbor as yourself.

As the now irresistible L-current continues to clear your inner and outer vision, you will see your neighbor, regardless of the role he is playing, in a new light. You will see that your neighbor is always a representative of love whether he appears as friend or enemy, member of your family, coworker, boss, employee, marriage partner, divorce partner, challenge, or inspiration. Your neighbor comes into your world to work *with* you—to pat you on the back, to encourage you, to praise you, to inspire you to live up to your highest potential. Your neighbor also comes into your world to work *on* you—to call to your attention, often in irritating, baffling, and frustrating ways, deficiencies in your makeup, make you aware of blind spots in your consciousness, bring to your attention the often deep-seated and subtle forms of bondage such as spiritual pride, smugness, and complacency. You will be realizing that you are in love with every neighbor, that every association with another person is an association in love, and that every relationship must ultimately be handled in love. You will see with startling clarity that no relationship is complete until it is completed in love, that you are never freed from any relationship until you are freed in love, that no relationship has served its purpose until it has served its purpose in love. If you have been "looking for a god with skin on," relax friend, cease your labor. You have found it in yourself and in your neighbor. Your new insight and your growing ability to see yourself and your neighbor in this new light are indispensable elements in learning to love your neighbor as yourself.

# XIX

# LET YOUR NEIGHBOR LOVE YOU

There are times during our unfoldment in love when we expect the world to stand still so we can love it on our terms. We may not realize yet that love is not only giving, it is also receiving. To love our neighbor as ourself also means to let him love us. To let our neighbor love us requires just as much love, life, light, and laughter as loving him.

When a loving woman minister (my wife) left one group to take up a new assignment in another area, a member of the congregation came up to her and said, "Thank you for loving us and for letting us love you. I feel that you really and truly loved all of us, but you are also willing to let us love you in our own way—and that must have been a real challenge at times!"

Just the thought that we are to let others love us as we love them is a breathtaking insight. It opens up a whole new dimension in the adventure of love. There are those to whom loving others and giving to others become a matter of spiritual pride, and it often represents a narrow attitude and constricting inlook and outlook on life. Have you ever heard the expression, "I love to give, but I don't really want or expect anything from others." Maybe you have even felt some of these elements within yourself. It can be rather pleasing to the ego to feel that we are "a big shot" (or, as my Nigerian friends phrase it so beautifully, "a big gun") in love. We can feel pretty important if we mistakenly assume that we are the only one who has the opportunity, right, or privilege to bring love, life, light, and laughter into our world. We may be so busy loving, doing good, living for others that we engulf them in a blind stream of busy affection that gives them no opportunity to try their own wings of self-expression in love. We can become so preoccupied with "doing our thing" that we forget our neighbor needs to do "his own thing" also. We are not really loving our neighbor as ourself until we give him the opportunity to be himself, and to be alert and responsive enough to encourage him to do exactly that.

We often see, especially in the relationship between parents and other adults and children, how the individuality and uniqueness of a child are literally drowned in the flood of supposedly loving concern, advice, and gifts that are poured into, over, and around him. Love-professing adults are often so busy "doing their thing," which often includes living the child's life for him, that he is never given the opportunity to find and express himself.

I have been blessed by having a handsome, strong-willed, and alert grandson. Once when he was still at the learning-to-talk-walk-and-climb stage, he and I were off somewhere in a hurry, as is so often the case. He had just discovered the thrill of climbing up into the car by himself, and on this day I felt I was too rushed to give him that opportunity. So I reached down to grab him by the seat of the pants and toss him into the car, but he would have none of it. He turned around and stopped me in midaction with these firm words. "No, Datz, Ricky do it!" In spite of my hurry, we both looked at each other for a startled moment and then burst out laughing. The half minute or so he needed to get into the car in his own way was time well invested for both of us.

It often takes time, patience, and energy, which we may assume unlovingly we do not have, to give others the opportunity to express themselves, do things in their own way, exercise their individuality and uniqueness, and yet is not this often our greatest act of love—to give another the gift of giving himself, being himself, sharing himself, reaching into the treasure of his own heart and uniqueness and sharing it with us? Is there any way to measure the gift that we share with our world when we learn to be good receivers as well as enthusiastic givers? Love not only gives of itself, it receives of itself. Love is never limited to just giving or just receiving, and neither are we as we learn to live in love. To receive without giving is to become a stagnant Dead Sea of being—but to give without receiving is to become empty, sterile, and separated from the stream of life. Life is the circulation system of love, and he who is truly alive in love receives as freely as he gives and gives as freely as he receives.

Have you ever watched the sparkle of love, life, light, and laughter that came into a child's eyes as he gave you some grimy treasure from his grimy horde of special gifts? You could give him no greater gift than to accept the one he held out in his tiny hand. And how often we may have made it difficult for a child (and we are all children in love) to find and express himself because we were too busy and unloving to accept his gift of time, love, and inexperience.

Can you imagine what Jesus did for the harlot when he accepted her gift of precious ointment, the touch of her supposedly sin-stained hands and hair, the tears that fell from her eyes? What do you suppose he did for the fellow who supplied the donkey on which he rode into the city of Jerusalem? The man who supplied the room for the Lord's Supper? Or even the man who built the cross? Or who drove the nails? Or the thieves on the cross whose suffering he accepted as his own? Or the man who let him use his tomb?

In the adventure of learning to love your neighbor, give him the opportunity to love you. Take the time to let him be himself in your presence and in his relationships with you. Let him be himself. Encourage him to be himself. Establish yourself in the atmosphere of love which invites him to be himself, even if it means radical growth for you in love and understanding and appreciation.

I was once called upon to conduct a rather unusual funeral service. The guest of honor—and I always feel that the one who has just departed from the range of our outer vision is the guest of honor—had requested that the love songs recorded by Frank Sinatra be played as a background throughout the entire service. The funeral director and some members of the family were concerned that I might be concerned. When I was asked if it would be all right with me, love in me responded with the words, "That's just fine with me. He is a unique individual, so let him preserve that uniqueness. Even in the experience we have labeled death, I can appreciate an individual who exercises his individuality to the so-called end. His request is also evidence to me of the immortality of the soul, because the spirit of this fellow is right with us and active in this service." I will have to admit that it wasn't the easiest service I have ever conducted, but I feel it was one of the most rewarding for me and the members of his family and the circle of his friends who were present.

It may seem easy to see that we should let our neighbor be himself, to share his gift of love, if it is a good one and he is a good person, or at least subscribes to our way of looking at things. But what of those who are still so caught up in fear, so ignorant of their true nature that they strike out with violence and destructive acts. Does not this attitude, if adopted, make us a door mat on which the world wipes its feet?

We become a door mat and the world wipes its feet on us when we permit what happens to unbutton us emotionally—to release the old reactions of fear, condemnation, and vindictiveness. The revelation is that we are not to resist evil but that we are to love our enemies. When we meet fear with fear, more fear is the result, and we become victimized by the fear we are fighting or resisting. When we love, we are the master of self and its actions. When we fear we are the victim of self and its reactions. No problem is solved at the level of consciousness that produced it. When we accept appearances at face value and judge by them, on that basis, we are the victims.

We are learning from actual inner experience that our old fearful reactions and negative states of thought and feeling can be dissolved by exposure to the L-current of love, life, light, and laughter. Our growing experience in love gives us insight into how to help our neighbor release some of his load of fear, hatred, and condemnation, if he happens to be in such a state. As we remain anchored in our dwelling place of love, our neighbor will be freed from some of the bonds of fear and inner anguish, even if we do no more than simply walk by each other on the street. If we are called into a more intimate or even violent type of confrontation, our awareness of love in operation will have a calming and beneficial influence. You certainly know people, as I do, who have such a strong sense of love that just to come into their presence is to feel at peace and be freed from irritation and unhappiness. You, too, are becoming such a person to the degree that the L-current of love, life, light, and laughter is expanding its operation in you, through you, and as you.

There is no rigid format to follow. You are discovering that you cannot rehearse or plan in advance what you are going to do in various situations and relationships. As love takes over in your mind and heart, you find more and more opportunities for it to operate. Strangers will come up to you and begin to empty their hearts and their minds. Old friends will detect a new dimension in you, even if they do not comment on it. Even the plants and animals in your life will respond to what is taking place in you.

Most of us are not going to be called upon to face the extremely violent fear reactions of the emotionally disturbed and mentally unbalanced. We are not likely to be nailed to the cross as Jesus was, or have to face the assassin's bullets as did Lincoln, Gandhi, the Kennedys, or Martin Luther King. We will be called upon, though, to meet the daily challenges and opportunities of living with people in the ordinary relationships of life, and, in a sense, this may prove to be even more challenging than one great dramatic act of laying down our life for all humanity. Life, as someone has observed, "is so daily." Moment-by-moment, event-by-event living calls for a loving, alert, joyous discipline that keeps us on our spiritual toes constantly. It is wonderful to realize that as we love our neighbor and let him love us at the levels of consciousness where we are now growing and unfolding, we are making a contribution to the universal good of mankind. We are discovering that the violence and war that plague mankind at international levels are only the sum total of the war and violence that go on in individuals. On a more positive note, the love and peace and ultimate freedom that humanity will realize is the sum total of the love, peace, and freedom that operate in individuals.

Even if a neighbor is in such fear and darkness that his violent acts threaten destruction on such a scale that you have to participate in restraining him in outer ways, you need not participate in the fear and anguish that have captured him. You need not be partner to an act of punishment or vindictiveness. You can act in love and from love, and you will add by your act to the light in the world, not to the darkness.

Society and nations, as well as individuals, are discovering that they do not solve their problems by punishing and killing their enemies—they only add to their problems with this approach. Every enemy is ultimately to be overcome in, by, and with love. Even nations that apparently emerged as victors in war soon find that they are confronted with a more ruthless, capable, and implacable foe than ever before. This has happened throughout all history and includes the Roman Empire, the British Empire, the Germans, the Americans, the Russians, the Chinese, and it will continue to include all nations who draw the sword to handle their enemies.

Shortly after the first atomic bombs were dropped, Gandhi pointed out that it was too early yet to determine what would happen to the soul of the nation that dropped the first atomic bomb on humanity. It is pretty obvious that the soul of that nation is required to go through a purging that will free it from the fearful reactions that caused it to move as it did—and by that purging to help free other nations and peoples of the world from the same fearful reactions. We are one internationally as well as individually, and love is no respecter of persons, nations, societies, or peoples. We are all to come under its dominion and be operated by it.

Jesus even had to restrain his overzealous disciples. Once when a city failed to give them the reception the disciples thought they deserved, they implored Jesus to follow the example of Elijah and call down fire from heaven to consume their enemies. But Jesus lovingly refused, telling them that they did not yet understand the nature of the spirit they were called to serve. As we move along the pathway of light, we discover that we are to let our light shine, not use it to belt our enemies over the head. In love we are no longer forced to live fearfully in each other's shadow—we can grow in each other's light.

We are discovering that no one has a corner on the truth. The truth is a great circle that includes everyone, and each one has some of the love and the life of the Infinite within him, regardless of his present state of unfoldment. We can no longer afford the luxury, and an expensive luxury it was, to believe and feel that we are all right and everyone else is all wrong. On his deathbed, a wonderful friend said to me, "Sig, all my life I have looked at life in terms of black and white, right and wrong. I can see, now that I am about ready to leave this world, that there is a lot of gray between that black and white." I might add that, in addition to that gray, there is a lot of technicolor. We are really coming into a technicolor age in the beliefs and attitudes in man.

The individuals and groups who profess to be concerned with the soul of man certainly present a varied and colorful scene. In their ranks we have the religious fundamentalists, semifundamentalists and antifundamentalists. We have the Catholics, the Protestants, the New Thoughters, and the Metaphysicians. We have the Pentecostalists, the speakers in tongues, the Jesus People, the Jesus "freaks," the Jesus de-freakers. We have Scripture-quoting, Bible-toting, pulpit-pounding evangelists—somber, sober theologians—and, at the other extreme, Satan worshipers. We have psychologists, psychiatrists, doctors, scientists. We have Mohammedans, Buddhists, Sufis. We have psychics, palm readers, astrologers. We have orange-robed monks, bearded gurus, soothsayers, the "viewers with alarm," the viewers with hope. We have the negative thinkers, the positive thinkers—oh, what a technicolor bowl of assistance the soul of man is going through right now; and we are called upon to meet and greet them all in the spirit of love, life, light, and laughter. Through our inner search and experience we are realizing that God, the Infinite Spirit of love, life, light, and joy, is bigger than all the opinions and revelations of the divine nature added together and multiplied a million billion times. No doubt in the transcendent purpose of infinite love, each element, individual, or group has its own role to play, and while we may find that many of the concepts presented are to us somewhat (to lift a word from the fertile vocabulary of my colleague Dr. Ernest C. Wilson) "underwhelming," we can stand relatively undisturbed in the integrity of our growing love awareness. We might even take the stand adopted by the wise, loving Gamaliel in the days when Christianity was still a cult. He suggested to the headstrong and intolerant of his day, to put it in the vernacular: "Take it easy, boys. Don't be too hard on this new cult, or you may find yourself on the wrong side of the fence. You may even wind up opposing God."

I like the attitude of the Kahuna priest who told me in Hawaii a few years ago that he had never met a man who didn't teach him something (I have long been intrigued by the connection between "cult" and "culture." Our culture seems to be made up of "cults" that stayed around long enough to become respectable, formidable, and prosperous!), and the attitude of Will Rogers, who was so conscious of the love current that he had never met a man he didn't like.

It may be necessary to remind ourselves occasionally of the revelation of Jesus, who in his sermon on what I like to call the Mount of Love, pointed out that "anyone who looks down on his brother as a lost soul is himself heading for the fire of destruction." As the L-current of love, life, light, and laughter continues its operation in us, we can see why this must be so. If we condemn another or think of him as a lost soul or a lost cause, we are setting up within ourselves the destructive fire of fear, hate, and condemnation, and we are also indicating that we do not think too much of the universal Creative Spirit of love, life, light, and laughter, if we do not give it credit for being able to save, unfold, and resurrect its own.

Perhaps we are ready to enter that state of love described by Albert Schweitzer: "I must regard other life than my own with equal reverence, for I shall know that it longs for fullness and

## LET YOUR NEIGHBOR LOVE YOU

development as deeply as I do myself. Therefore, I see that evil is what annihilates, hampers, or hinders life. Goodness, by the same token, is saving or helping life, the enabling of whatever life I can influence, to obtain its highest development." Certainly we are coming to that point in our own love unfoldment where we realize that a God of love or a humanity of love could not live in peace if even one of its members was excluded from love. We are all one family, the children of one God. If all humanity except one poor soul were saved and he was stuck in some pit of hell, I am sure that saved humanity would rush from its preferred spot in heaven and surround that soul in that pit of hell so completely with love, life, light, and laughter that both the soul and hell would be resurrected. Richard Bach, who checked out the love and flight potential of the seagull, found that even heaven could not hold the gull that had entered the light, so long as there were any members of the family who needed help on the earth. The eagle had to rescue his brother from the chicken yard, and no soul can rest until every other soul in the human family is at peace in the love of the Creator.

I think you will enjoy the following exchange from newspaper columnist Ann Landers. She expresses beautifully and simply the everlasting brotherhood and unity of man. "Dear Ann Landers: You owe your readers an apology for saying: 'All men are brothers in the family of God. This would make Al Capone a brother to Pope John.' Well, I don't want Al Capone for a brother and I don't think you ought to give him to Pope John, either. Some writers don't care what they say so long as they get paid for it.—Fed Up With You. Dear Fed: The accurate wording was, 'We are all brothers in the family of man.' However, if you believe that God is the father of all mankind, you must then believe that all men are brothers. Even Al Capone and Pope John."

Does not the shepherd of love leave the "ninety and nine" who have entered the heaven of love to search for the one who has yet to return home? Would not you, in your present state of awareness, do the same?

Anyway, since man is the image of God, the individualized

spirit of love, life, light, and laughter, there is really no hell that can contain him forever. Eventually he would joyously come to himself and, with all that energy available, would figure out some way to air-condition the place. He would return to the Father's house and by that time perhaps even the sulking son who stayed home would have received enough enlightenment from the L-current to join in the welcome.

Sometimes I am asked if I believe in hell and I say, "Yes, I have been in it many times," but like the explorer of old, I am beginning to realize that even in hell "thou art with me." Others ask if I believe in heaven, and I say, "Yes, I run in and out of it all the time, but one of these days when I enter it, I plan to stay in accordance with the promise that that will happen." We are discovering that every time we leave love, every time we let the reaction of fear move us out of our true dwelling place, we are in hell. And every time we return to our dwelling place in love, we are in heaven.

Perhaps the idea or realization in the following words will describe, in some measure at least, the experience we are sharing:

*I congratulate the universal Creative Spirit of love, life, light, and laughter on the miracle on waking me up. I am delighted by my growing ability to love my neighbor as myself—and not only to love him, but to let him love me. I am grateful for the growing sense of unity with all humanity, that love has established and is expanding in me.*

## XX

# DEVELOP YOUR "LQ"

In a conversation with a friend one day about the project of how to love your neighbor, he said, "It sounds to me, Sig, as if you are trying to help people develop their 'LQ'—or their 'Love Quotient.'" I like the sound of that, don't you? We have lived through an age or cycle in human unfoldment when the "IQ," or "Intelligence Quotient," has been held in high regard, and of course it is extremely important. We are now moving from the head, or intellect, to the heart, or love, faculty in human potential. Our IQ is certainly high enough, so that we can readily see how important it is to develop our LQ. Love is not only a dwelling place, a creative energy field; it is also a faculty, talent, and potential in man. Its development is undoubtedly a great deal like the development of other faculties in human consciousness such as color perception, the musical or artistic sense, and many others. These faculties probably become active in a few individuals first, and then eventually permeate all of human consciousness, just as yeast permeates the whole pan of dough. The love faculty has been slow to awaken in humanity as a whole, although it is active to some degree in everyone. The universal Creative Spirit of love, life, light, and laughter is not going to be satisfied until all of its children, its sons and daughters, become the self-expression of the mighty L-current.

It has been interesting to see how this manuscript has taken on a life and direction of its own. It does not always move in the direction that I consciously feel it will. Also, in sharing some of the ideas in the book with members of my family, friends, and others who for one reason or another know of the project, it seems that many of the ideas take root and immediately begin to grow and expand. The fourfold gospel of love, life, light, and laughter has taken a jump in me, and I can see now that it is rapidly becoming a sevenfold, or seven-faceted, activity.

To the four elements of love, life, light, and laughter, I now add *loyalty, letting,* and *liberty*. As our real self begins to stand up on its feet and take over in mind, heart, body, and life experience, it inspires a deep loyalty. I am reminded of a statement that a minister in a church I attended some years ago used to make nearly every Sunday: "Be loyal to the royal that is within you." There is a royal spirit within each one of us—our real self. And of course we have discovered this same royal spirit, this real self of love, life, light, and laughter, in our neighbor as well. Probably in one form or another we are taking an oath of loyalty, a pledge of allegiance to this spirit of royalty that we are discovering in ourself and in our neighbor. We are giving up some of our old loyalties, the pledges of allegiance we have made to our fearful, or reactionary, self, and we no longer hang on so tightly to the old attitudes that ruled us. This loyalty is a spontaneous response to the wonderful new state of selfhood that we are entering. We might say that our loyalty is our response ability, our ability to respond to our real self. We will eventually give up our loyalty to our lesser states of selfhood and have no other "gods" before our real self. We will extend this loyalty to our neighbor also; or, to put it another way, we will love, revere, worship, respect, and appreciate the self of love, life, light, and laughter that we are coming to know in ourself and in our neighbor.

You will find from actual experience that you are entering into that state of mind and heart, that inner attitude that might be described in the following words:

*I am loyal to the royal within me. I am true to my inner self of love, life, light, and laughter.*

It may be that this realization will come to you in the midst of an experience or situation that might tempt you to return to some old and outgrown state of selfhood. You will rejoice as you consciously make the choice to "be loyal to the royal" within.

You will also, through actual experience, come to the state where you realize that where your neighbor is concerned you can say accurately:

*I am loyal to the royal within my neighbor. I am true to his inner self of love, life, light, and laughter.*

This, too, may come through an experience or situation in which you were tempted to believe that your neighbor was once again the victim of an old fearful state of mind and heart, but you consciously chose to "be loyal to the royal" within him. You will be thrilled to realize that you have used your response ability, your ability to respond to your neighbor in a loving, dynamic, and creative way. As you practice being "loyal to the royal" within yourself and your neighbor, you will be developing your LQ, and you will be loving your neighbor as yourself.

You will undoubtedly be able to see that many of your old loyalties arose out of fear, but that your new loyalty is rooted and grounded in love, nourished by life, illumined by light, and strengthened by joy. Only the real self of humanity in you and in your neighbor is worthy of your unswerving loyalty. Your response ability, your ability to respond to the reality within you and your neighbor, will continue to grow.

As your ability to "be loyal to the royal" in you and your neighbor grows, you will be taking another great step toward freedom, or liberty. This is the step of letting. We must ultimately let this royal self within reveal its own infinite nature. We will discover how true it is that the selfhood prepared for us has not yet entered our minds and hearts. It is not circumscribed by our concepts and opinions. It has plans, intentions, talents, and energies of its own. "As the heavens are higher than the earth," its potentialities are greater than anything we have conceived during our fearful states of self-experience. Eventually we will stop trying to tell this real inner self what it is and let it reveal its own nature in us and in our neighbor. This attitude of letting develops our LQ. Love always lets its creation be what it is created to be, a self-expression of love. In many ways this is the most difficult step on the road to liberty in love. The IQ complex has been in the saddle so long it is hard to realize that something greater is on the scene. The IQ is loath to admit that it must decrease and that the LQ must increase. This, of course, does not mean that the IQ actually decreases, its authority has to be yielded. Or, to put it in another way, the intellect has to be ruled by love. The time is at hand when "the government will be upon his shoulders." Love is to be the ruling energy in the consciousness of humanity, and nobody really knows what love is. We are agreed that it is the most powerful and creative and desirable energy in the universe. The enlightened IQs are saying that love's time has come. Now all we have to do is to let it take over in our own minds and hearts, let it begin its reign in us, become love's self-expression.

Those who live in the revelation of love will come to know the truth, and the truth will set them free. When we know the truth that we are the self-expression of love, life, light, and laughter, that truth will set us free by making us a Spiritual Independent, a new creature and a new creation. We will discover through actual experience the truth that "where the spirit of the Lord is, there is liberty," the glorious liberty of the awakening sons and daughters of the Infinite. As you catch the vision and the feeling of this liberty, the liberty of the Creative Spirit of love, life, light, and laughter that you truly are, you will be not only developing the LQ, but the LQ will take over and develop you. Love is not an energy, a power, a tool that you can use to "feather your own nest." And the more you develop your LQ the more love takes over in your heart, soul, mind, and life. As Kahlil Gibran puts it so beautifully, "And think not you can direct the course of love, for love, if it finds you worthy, directs your course." Love finds you worthy when it finds you willing to become its self-expression; when you surrender your whole being to its life, light, laughter; when you are loyal to its awakening self in you and in your neighbor; when you let it unfold its nature; when you accept the liberty that is yours as an offspring of infinite love.

## DEVELOP YOUR "LQ"

As the liberty and freedom of love begin to unfold in your consciousness, you may well feel as if you were emerging from a dark tunnel of fear and limitation. And of course that is exactly what is happening. You are emerging from the darkness of fear, the blind bondage to conformity and rebellion, the smog of ignorance and superstition; you are coming into the light of your inner self, and for a time you may well feel that you are "a stranger in paradise." You have been penned up and boxed in. Now you are free, free to be a Spiritual Independent, a magnificent awakening creature of love, life, light, and laughter. You are at liberty to join the awakening sons and daughters of the Infinite, to be loyal to your real self and let your inner self reveal its infinite nature of love.

When I was a youngster I lived on ranches and farms in North Dakota and Montana, where the winters were pretty severe. For the most part, we had to keep our animals, our cows and horses, in barns and shelters, and one of the most delightful times was that day in spring when we finally turned them out into the pasture. They would come out into the barnyard, often blinking at the unaccustomed, brilliant light. Some of the calves and colts almost immediately began to run around and kick their heels in delight, shaking the kinks out of unused muscles. Even the older animals were ultimately stirred to a sense of freedom and joined in the spring dance. All creation seemed to be singing, "It's time to wake up, come alive, enter into the glorious experience of life that love has prepared for all its creatures."

As you emerge from the wintry tunnel of fear and move into the springtime of your own soul, you will find the welcome mat out from all creation. You will be able to share in the feeling of St. Paul, who wrote: "The whole creation is on tiptoe to see the wonderful sight of the sons of God coming into their own. The world of creation cannot as yet see reality, not because it chooses to be blind, but because in God's purpose it has been so limited—yet it has been given hope. And the hope is that in the end, the whole of created life will be rescued from the tyranny of change and decay, and have its share in that magnificent liberty which can only belong to the children of God." You are part of the cutting edge of this great stage of creative evolution. You are not playing for small stakes in learning to love, accept, and believe in yourself as a Spiritual Independent. You are a sovereign individual, a son (or daughter) of God coming into your own, a conscious self-expression of the love, life, light, and laughter that make up your real nature. You are at least on the threshold of a new birth in selfhood, and while at present perhaps all you know is a fraction of your true self, the time and the experience will inevitably come when you will know it as fully as your Creator does. It is high time that we all leave the dark and the wintry tunnel and draw a deep breath in the fresh atmosphere of love. As Thomas Moore phrases it so beautifully:

> When "from the lips of truth" one mighty breath
> Shall like a whirlwind scatter in its breeze
> That whole dark pile of human mockeries—
> Then shall the reign of mind commence on earth,
> And starting fresh as from a second birth,
> Man in the sunshine of the world's new spring
> Shall walk transparent like some holy thing!

The "one mighty breath from the lips of truth" that will clear the shrouds of fear, guilt, condemnation, and unhappiness from our soul and mind is the mighty L-current developing and expanding our LQ. As your LQ develops, you can even look back into the wintry tunnel of darkness and rejoice in all its experiences. You will see that your entire life has been part of a creative plan that has led you to this point of self-acceptance and self-realization. You could, or you would, come "no other way," as Martha Smock, editor of *Daily Word*, points out so beautifully in her poem:

> Could we but see the pattern of our days,
> We should discern how devious were the ways
> By which we came to this, the present time,
> This place in life; and we should see the climb

## DEVELOP YOUR "LQ"

Our soul has made up through the years.
We should forget the hurts, the wanderings, the fears,
The wastelands of our life, and know
That we could come no other way or grow
Into our good without these steps our feet
Found hard to take, our faith found hard to meet.
The road of life winds on, and we like travelers go
From turn to turn until we come to know
The truth that life is endless and that we
Forever are inhabitants of all eternity.

So here we are, my wonderful awakening friend, on the threshold of spiritual independence, conscious in growing measure of the mighty L-current of love, life, light, and laughter entering the liberty, the freedom of self-expression, for which we are created. Our LQ is growing, it is unfolding its selfhood as us, and while we are just beginning to discover the dimensions of our spirit, at least we are under way.

Perhaps you may wish to flex your spiritual wings a bit by moving into the experience outlined in the following words:

*Every time I exercise my LQ I enjoy it more, I do it better, and I am stronger, livelier, and freer than ever before.*

Or,

*Every time I lovingly assert my spiritual independence, I enjoy it more, I do it better, and I am freer, more creative, more adventurous than ever before.*

Or,

*Every time I am loyal to my real self, I enjoy it more, I do it better, and I am healthier, freer, and more loving than ever before.*

Or—whatever the rapidly expanding LQ in you inspires you to do.

In the title of his splendid book, Eric Butterworth joyously points out that *Life Is for Loving.* How true this is, as we are learning from actual experience. And also, as we are learning from actual experience, "Love Is for Living." Love is your real nature, and as you discover this, you get a new lease on life because love dramatically increases your options for living. The courses of creative action that are open to you in your inner and outer world as your LQ increases your life potential and experience, are dramatically expanded. "Love Is for Living." You know it and you show it by the way you think, feel, speak, and act. You are becoming a Spiritual Independent, a dynamic, adventurous creature of love, life, light, and laughter. You are a Spiritual Independent, your LQ is growing, the mighty L-current is expanding its operation in you, through you, and as you, and you are exercising the options that love gives you with growing confidence, joy, and enthusiasm. You are increasingly "loyal to the royal" in yourself and in your neighbor, and you are experiencing and sharing the liberty which the whole universe is tiptoe-ready to receive!

## XXI

# THE OPTIONS OF LOVE

"Love is for living"—and we have been discovering through actual experience that love gives us a new lease on life, new ways to see God, ourself, our neighbor, our world; new options and courses of action to meet the challenges and opportunities that constantly confront us in our inner and outer world; new choices of thought and feeling; new insights into the nature of the Creator and of the creative process in us. We are discovering that our desire for greater self-expression in love is the desire of love for greater self-expression through us. We have met and are being taken over by the impact energy of love that often jars the even tenor of our ways, knocks electrons off our tight little atoms of living, and leaves us startled, gasping, growing. "Love is for living"—we are coming alive in love and love is coming alive in us, and I feel that we are sharing in a deepening realization that has been thrilling me for years.

> "God is love,"
> and in that love
> we live and move and have our being!
> What a tremendous, joyous, freeing
> (it makes my soul sing!)
> to know and feel
> that I am in love
> with everyone and everything.

"Love is for living"—and as we move more deeply into love and love moves more deeply and powerfully in us, we discover that in love there are worlds beyond worlds beyond worlds, and heavens beyond heavens beyond heavens—there are depths beyond depths beyond depths, and heights beyond heights beyond heights—there are glories beyond glories beyond glories, and joys beyond joys beyond joys—there are ins beyond ins beyond ins, and outs beyond outs beyond outs—we discover that with each awakening thrust our soul makes into the infinity that is love, we are transcending our old states of selfhood, being moved by new currents of energy, becoming new creatures in love, life, light, and laughter.

We are discovering something of the nature of love and therefore of life. While we can never confine it or really define it in words, it is sometimes helpful to do so for our own illumination. Sometimes I am asked if I write books and I say honestly, "No, I write myself. If what I write turns up in a book, that is fine with me and I hope it will be an inspiration to someone else." No doubt some of the ideas in the following lines have occurred to you many times.

## LOVE

And what shall I say of Love?
It is more like a discovery
    than a set of rules.
It is more like music
    than arithmetic.
It is more like inspiration
    than instruction.
It is more like electricity
    than creed or doctrine.
It is more like sunshine
    than a moral code.
It is more like rain
    than law and order.
It is more like joy
    than duty.

## THE OPTIONS OF LOVE

When one becomes love in action
he moves from the law
 of Karma
to the miracle of grace—
from reaping what he sows
to harvesting what he is—
 what God IS—
 what the universe is.

The more you deal with love, or the more love deals with you, the more you will realize that the activity of love is to educate the heart, your emotional and feeling nature. Our head, or intellect, is probably overeducated and overinflated by its own sense of importance. Intellectually we may know that we should love our neighbor, that it is foolish to hate and condemn and fear, but emotionally very few have attained that degree of maturity. So love does its primary work in the heart. Love is true feeling, true emotion. Love is the feeling of oneness shared with the Creator and creation, and ultimately love is the feeling that creation returns to the Creator. As you work with the options of love, which we will now consider, you will discover that, while they have intellectual dimensions, their primary and most fulfilling area of activity is in the feeling nature. To know the truth that sets us free we must really feel it. Love is fulfilled, brought to earth, as it is put into practice in our emotions, in the relationships and experiences of daily living.

Let's take a look at some of the options that love gives us in the everyday, down-to-earth experiences in living. Any one of these options obviously can be expanded into a book, a permanent attitude, a way of life. To these options you can add many that are becoming apparent to you. Love always works in this way—it is constantly opening up new options of living, new choices in the way we will go inwardly and outwardly. Love never says, "Stay where you are." It says, "Start where you are. Make your choice of the options I offer to you and move into new and creative experiences in living."

## HOW TO LOVE YOUR NEIGHBOR

The first great option that love gives us is the opportunity to change our dwelling place. Even if we are in a deep pit of hell, or boxed into some torture chamber of fear, or tied into knots by some element of conformity or rebellion, or stretched out in some upholstered rut of complacency and inertia, love always extends the option and the invitation to return to its dynamic energy fields of life, light, and laughter. Love always urges us to wake up and surrender to the mighty L-current, to let our LQ be expanded, and to experience a glorious liberty that belongs to a Spiritual Independent. This would seem to be such a wonderful, easy, and logical option to take up, but as you are discovering from actual experience, it is quite a project. Nonetheless, let's resolve now to take this option of changing our dwelling place with confidence, joy, and enthusiasm.

Step consciously right now into the dwelling place of love, realize that you are surrounded, imbedded in, and permeated by creative energy fields in which there is no darkness, fear, guilt, condemnation, limitation. Then let your consciousness expand so that you can get the feeling of being in love with your neighbor, your world, your work, your own potential as a self-expression of love. Wherever you happen to be reading this book, take a moment to remind yourself, "I am in love right now." Even if you are in a room alone, be in love with the furniture, the walls, the books, the floor, the ceiling, and you will immediately begin to see and feel new dimensions of your surroundings and, of course, of yourself. Practice living in love, no matter where you are or with whom you happen to be. As love clears your consciousness and your vision, you will begin to see the universe and the creatures in it as they truly are and you will be moving into a new and creative way of life.

A number of years ago one of our sons, who was in his early teens, had a date with a young lady who, in his estimation at the time, was considerably younger and therefore not quite entitled to his time and attention. It was one of those pressure dates that parents are likely to inflict upon their sons and daughters. I suggested to him that he adopt the attitude that whenever he is with a girl whether she is seven, seventeen, seventy, or "seventy times seven," that he try to realize he is in love with her. She is therefore entitled to his love simply because they are in love together, and he can relax and give her his undivided interest and attention. He can enjoy and appreciate her for what she is and not be unhappy because for the moment he is not with some other girl who might come closer to his specifications. I also pointed out that this principle would apply regardless of the sex of the person with whom love had brought him together. A few years later he told me, "Dad, this being in love with everyone you meet certainly makes for an interesting way of life!"

Check it out for yourself with the members of your family, your coworkers, employers, employees, strangers on the street. If you happen to be on an airplane or in a restaurant, remind yourself that you are in love with the people immediately at hand and that in that love there is nothing but life, light, joy, interest, and mutual appreciation. You will be amazed at how the entire situation changes. Sometimes waitresses or waiters in a restaurant can serve us for an hour or two, anticipating and responding to our needs and desires, and we might not even realize what they are wearing, what the color of their eyes is, whether they are happy or sad, tall or short! When it comes time to pay the check, we may even have difficulty remembering who our waitress or waiter is. We failed to take up the option of living in love with another human being for a portion of eternity, and who is to measure what this oversight cost us and the waitress or waiter in the riches that love constantly offers to all who are willing and alert enough to live in it? Living in love is a fantastic exercise that brings immediate and lasting results.

Perhaps most of the time we are not so much with people as we are with our opinions of people. We tend to see people through opinionated vision, and we often fail to appreciate what they really are because we are not loving enough to let them be themselves, free themselves, express themselves completely in our presence. This is another option that love extends to us—to appreciate others for what they are. We are told that "possession is nine points of the law," but in love, all the points go to appreciation. In our progress in love we move from intolerance through tolerance to appreciation. Intolerance and tolerance are two sides of the same coin of fear. To be tolerant is not enough. Have you ever been tolerated by members of your family, by adults when you were a child, or by members of a supposedly superior religion, race, or social group? Then you know from personal experience what I mean. Love is neither intolerant nor tolerant. Love appreciates.

When we love, everything in the inner and outer universe belongs to us by right of appreciation. We hold no other title to anyone or anything. Does not a child belong more completely to a loving teacher who appreciates him than to thoughtless parents who merely tolerate him because he "belongs" to them through a blood relationship? Many a husband and wife have awakened to the shocking realization that their spouses belong more completely to a loving, appreciative friend than to them, even though they may have retained legal title through a marriage license or certificate.

In other fields we find that no one can get a corner on or possess the truth, or those individuals through whom the truth revelation comes. I have a wonderful friend in Kansas City, Rabbi William B. Silverman. We often refer to him as our "Unity Rabbi." One day when I did this he said, "Why shouldn't you call me the Unity Rabbi? After all, you stole the whole Unity movement from the Jews!" Laughingly I replied, "Bill, what do you mean? I didn't think anybody could steal anything from the Jews!" Bill came back promptly, "Doesn't the Old Testament say 'Hear, oh Israel, the Lord your God is one God.' Isn't that Unity?" The truth, no matter what label we put on it, is universal, and it belongs to anyone who loves it—that is, who appreciates it.

The same thing is true of the great souls, the enlightened ones, the saviors of the world. When our daughter was in grade school her best friend was a beautiful young Jewish girl. One day they went to a movie that featured the life and miracles of Jesus Christ. During the movie our daughter's friend became very excited and kept asking questions like, "Is that right? Did Jesus really do all those things?" Finally our daughter became quite impatient because she wanted to watch the movie, and she said, "What's the matter? Don't you know anything about Jesus?" "Of course," came back the prompt reply. "We studied all about him until he grew up and turned Catholic!"

Jesus not only grew up and turned Catholic, he grew some more and turned Protestant, and he grew some more and turned metaphysician, and he will continue to grow as more and more people appreciate him and his teaching and demonstration. The same thing is true of other great revelators of truth, including Mohammed, Buddha, Confucius, and many others. They cannot be neatly packaged, stamped with a label, and claimed by any group. They are the common, or we might say the *extraordinary*, property of all humanity, and they enter the minds, hearts, and lives of all who appreciate them.

Living in love, you have the option of being yourself rather than trying to please (or displease) others. You need no longer look for others' reactions before moving or acting on your own. You realize that you are a self-expression of the infinite Creative Spirit of love, life, light, and laughter, and you realize that being true to yourself is much more important than trying to please others.

Actually you have, no doubt, discovered that it is impossible to please others. You may do something one day that will please a person, but the next day something in his consciousness has changed and he is not pleased at all by the same action. Also, if any intelligent person catches you acting in a way simply because you are trying to please him, he will begin to suspect everything you do, because he will recognize that you are a "phony" or counterfeit and cannot be depended upon. The only way we can please anyone else is to be true to ourself. When we are true to ourself, even if someone else doesn't understand or accept completely what we do, we will have his respect because he will know that he has found that rarity, an honest human being.

In being true to ourself, we will undoubtedly come up against that old question, "What will people say?" Well, of this you can be sure. People will say what they are, or perhaps, more accurately, where they are in consciousness. The critics will say critical things. The fearful ones will say fearful things. The weak ones will say weak things. The gossipers will say gossipy things, and the loving ones will say loving things—each one will speak according to his own consciousness. But if you are true to yourself, that Creative Spirit of love, life, light, and laughter, everyone will eventually stop saying things to observe what you are doing. Some may even yield to the temptation to be true to themselves, and that's a delightful course of action to help initiate in others. The world has no alternative but to accept and to respect any person who is true to himself.

But you may ask, "What if being true to myself hurts others?" There is a saying, "There is no pain like champagne." Love is the champagne of all energy. There is no doubt that there is some pain involved in love. Kahlil Gibran suggests that if you can't let love take you to the threshing floor, you had better steer clear of it till you are ready. Former President Truman, referring to politics, had another suggestion: "If you can't stand the heat, stay out of the kitchen!" This does not mean that you deliberately set out to hurt yourself or others; on the other hand, love means growth, and growth quite often includes growing pains. Be true to yourself in a loving, lively, radiant, laughing way, knowing that love will be able to handle whatever growing pains it causes.

Start right now, in love, to be yourself. Express your desires, your feelings about even the small things in life. Since you are in love, you will not be doing this belligerently or trying to inflict your likes and desires upon other people. You are merely stating your case, letting your world know how you feel about things, expressing an attitude as valid as anyone else's. You may well find that your new, honest self will be accepted much more joyously and enthusiastically than was your old attempt to please people, to be concerned about what people might say, or to avoid hurting people. There may be an initial shock as you change your approach by living in love, but it will wear off, and others may decide to follow the same route in their own life. Love always gives us the option of a more interesting, creative, and adventurous way of life.

I know doctors who would never think of entering an operating room without taking time to affirm that the patient and everyone involved in the operation are *in love,* and that love's healing energies are on the job. I know businessmen who wouldn't think of going into a conference without first silently acknowledging that all the individuals involved are operating in an energy field of love, and that every transaction and decision is mutually profitable through the action of love. I know ministers who would never get up to speak to a congregation without silently acknowledging that the whole service is taking place in love, and that the power of the Holy Spirit of love moves in and through everyone to erase fear and stir up faith and joy. I know teachers who take the time every morning to acknowledge that every one of their students is a child of the Infinite and that their classrooms and the whole school where they work are filled with the love of the Infinite. I know nurses whose awareness of the omnipresent love can bring light to a whole hospital full of patients, nurses, doctors, visitors. I have met perfect strangers in a busy airport or on a city street (and in love every stranger is a *perfect* stranger!) whose awareness of the energy fields of love in which all humanity lives was so great that I could see and feel an ever-widening circle of light and peace flow out through them into the busy throng. These are the ones who have been caught up in the rapture of love—and is not this the promise that in the last days there would be two people sleeping together in bed and one would be caught up in love, there would be two working side by side in the field and one would become conscious of the miracle-working power of love and depart from the old activity of fear? Here and there and all around the globe, there would be those who are released from the paralysis of fear and lifted up into the growth and freedom of love? There are more and more people all the time who are exercising the infinite options of love in all their relationships, all their activities, all their work.

## HOW TO LOVE YOUR NEIGHBOR

All the books in the world and those yet to be written, couldn't possibly contain the options that love offers to those with the courage and desire to live in it.

The options of love are exercised in the smallest and most fleeting of contacts. While I was on a lecture tour in Switzerland with my wife, a charming experience occurred. My wife, our translator, and I had been meditating and talking all morning about living in love and what it meant. It was an early Sunday morning and we went out for a walk in the brisk breeze. Down the deserted street came a young woman. She was dressed in jeans and had long hair, and I suppose might be classified by some as a "hippie." She started to walk by us and then suddenly came over, threw her arms around me and kissed me on the cheek, said something in German, and moved swiftly on. Getting kissed on the cheek by a pretty woman is not exactly an unusual experience for a minister, but this was such a delightful, spontaneous, and pure experience that I have never forgotten it.

Another type of experience also comes to mind and heart. The first time I visited East Berlin was shortly after "the wall" was opened to visitors from the West. That was the time when buses and cars were being searched thoroughly by the East German guards. I was sitting at the bus window while it was stopped, and I was just a few feet away from a young East German soldier. He seemed completely frozen in the role he was carrying out. He reminded me of one of my own sons, and I looked at him intently, realizing almost unconsciously that in truth we were in love together. Suddenly he looked at me, his eyes unfroze, and a smile almost landed on his lips. Then suddenly he jerked himself out of love and assumed once again the role that had been drilled into him. But at least for a moment or two, love melted a section of the Berlin wall. That evening, after a lecture in Kongresse Halle, two or three persons, who still had members of their family on the east side of the wall, came up to me and said, "Thank you for having the courage to speak on love tonight. We know that only love can eventually melt the barriers that men have erected between themselves and other men. Even if the Berlin wall could be taken down by tanks and planes, it would go up again in some other city. Only love can permanently unite the hearts of men."

When I was thirteen years old, my brother and I were taking a bus trip. The bus stopped at a traffic intersection, and I looked out the window into the eyes of an attractive woman who was perhaps in her forties or fifties. Even though I wasn't conscious at that time that our real dwelling place is love, I will never forget the silent dialogue that passed between us. As we looked deep into each other's souls, I knew that I knew her, and I realized that she knew me and that she knew that she knew me and somehow I knew that we both knew; and I knew that she knew that we both knew. Then the bus lurched on, but the experience itself has never come to an end.

I don't know whether any of these three wonderful human beings and I will meet again in this lifetime, but I do know that we all shared an experience in love, and I have the feeling that we all know it. So over the invisible ribbons of love that link us, I send to them my gratitude and joy.

We live in a responsive universe and perhaps you, too, have come to the realization that I try to express in the following words:

### RESPONSE

I tried to conquer the universe
    and it defeated me—
I tried to understand the universe
    and it outwitted me—
I tried to capture the universe
    and it eluded me—
So, clumsily, hesitantly, I tried to
    love the universe
and it embraced me!

## HOW TO LOVE YOUR NEIGHBOR

Just the thought that love gives you an infinite number of options with which to meet the situations and the relationships in your life will work a miracle in you, in every relationship, the happy ones as well as the trying ones. You will find opportunities to carry out the options that love makes available to you, and hand in hand, mind in mind, heart in heart, we can move forward to the time foreseen by Maxim Gorky:

> There will come a time, I know, when people will take delight in one another, when each will be a star to the other, and when each will listen to his fellow as to music. The free men will walk upon the earth, men great in their freedom. They will walk with open hearts, and the heart of each will be pure of envy and greed, and therefore all mankind will be without malice, and there will be nothing to divorce the heart from reason. Then life will be one great service to man! His figure will be raised to lofty heights—for to free men all heights are attainable. Then we shall live in truth and freedom and in beauty, and those will be accounted the best who will the more widely embrace the world with their hearts, and whose love of it will be the profoundest; those will be the best who will be the freest; for in them is the greatest beauty. Then will life be great, and the people will be great who live that life.

Live in love, walk in love, love in love, exercise the options of love!

## XXII

## LOVE AND JUSTICE

"Yes, God is a God of love, but God is also a God of justice." This is a reminder that is always called to the attention of anyone who professes to serve the God of love—so let's take a look at justice. There are two versions of it available to all—the justice of fear and the justice of love. The justice of fear is always punishment, paralysis, bondage. The justice of love is always forgiveness, growth, freedom. As was pointed out by one who had delved deeply into the nature of love, fear always has to do with punishment, and love is not perfected in one who is fearful.

The greatest option of love is the option of forgiveness. Forgiveness is much more than excusing or pardoning. Forgiveness is the eternal activity of love, and it is always introducing an element of growth and a step toward greater freedom in the mind and heart of humanity. It operates in and through all the areas of human experience because, since it is the activity of love, it is as omnipresent as love itself. Forgiveness always reveals a new and higher way to move in growth and freedom.

It would seem that man would naturally choose the way of love, forgiveness, growth, and freedom rather than the bitter path of fear, punishment, paralysis and bondage—but history, for the most part, seems to prove otherwise. When the saviors of humanity have brought light, most men seem to have chosen to remain in the darkness of their fear, condemnation, superstition, and ignorance. Love, forgiveness, growth, and freedom have often been ignored. Instead of exercising the options of love, men have chosen to punish, paralyze, and bind themselves and others.

The option of forgiveness has to do with three elements in man's experience—his past, his present, and his future—that is, it is an eternal process. Without the option of forgiveness, love cannot operate. Love could never have created man except for the glorious truth that it is capable of forgiving him, growing him, and ultimately leading him into the freedom that belongs to him as an offspring of infinite love.

Perhaps you have read the conversation of Father God and Mother Nature before they decided to bring forth totally free creatures: men and women. The conversation is recorded in the memory banks of the universe, and if your imagination is alive and healthy, you can read it for yourself. The conversation goes something like this:

Father God: "Now that the rest of creation is finished, let us bring forth creatures in our own image and after our likeness—totally free creatures, and call them man and woman."

Mother Nature: "Dare we do this? Once we have done this thing, there is no backtracking. We are stuck with these free creatures forever."

Father God: "I think love is great enough to handle them."

Mother Nature: "Yes, in love we can forgive them, grow them, and ultimately free them in love."

Father God: "Is there any way our creative plan can be blocked?"

Mother Nature: "No, only through their own unforgiveness, their own reluctance to grow and unfold, can our family of humanity slow the process temporarily."

Thus it came to pass that those free-wheeling creatures, man and woman, came into being. Love has been forgiving them, growing them, freeing them for all eternity, overcoming their closed minds and hearts (the unforgivable sin), the reluctance to grow and unfold that which they really are—the spirit of love, life, light, and laughter.

## LOVE AND JUSTICE

Human history is filled with a record of those individuals who have chosen, consciously or unconsciously, to be instruments of forgiveness, the great option of love. In the life, teaching, demonstration, crucifixion, and resurrection of Jesus the Christ, we see the whole panorama of the forgiving activity of love at work. He brought the light of truth to earth, the truth that the kingdom of God is not in outer space but within men and women. He revealed that the nature of this kingdom is spirit—the spirit of love, life, light, and joy—and that one cannot enter this inner kingdom except through spiritual rebirth. Until we realize that we are spiritual beings, self-expressions of the universal spirit of love, life, light, and joy, we remain in the prison of fear, punishment, paralysis, and bondage. He urged that all men and women become perfect as the universal Creative Spirit is perfect—that is, all-inclusive in their love. His prayer from the cross for those who fearfully crucified him and all who still fear to follow him all the way, "Father forgive them, for they know not what they do," was answered and is still being answered, as all prayers for forgiveness are always answered. His resurrection from the dead tomb of fear, punishment, paralysis, and bondage was part of the answer, and the continuing activity of the current of love, life, and light that he released into the minds and hearts of humanity is still answering that prayer. I need not go into further detail on this, because you, who are living in love and letting that love dissolve the old states of human fear in your consciousness, know from actual experience what is taking place.

A friend of mine in Germany put his finger accurately on the forgiving activity of love in human consciousness right now when he told me, "Sig, the age of viciousness is coming to an end. The age of vicious human relationships, religion, politics, economics, racial practices, and fear is ending. The age of love and peace is being ushered into human experience; but in the process, as the old states of fear boil up from the subconsciousness of humanity, many who are ignorant of what is taking place will temporarily become victimized by it. But the result is inevitable. Love and peace will win out."

Now that your vision is clearing, you will see that throughout all human experience love has been able to work through those who have had the vision, faith, and courage to exercise the option of forgiveness. In the eternal heart of love, man has always been forgiven for every sin of his past, present, and future. Every fearful, ignorant, superstitious act on man's long and checkered pathway to light is already forgiven (not excused or pardoned) by the love that created him. Does this mean that man can continue in his acts of darkness, sin, and violence with impunity? No, of course not! Fear is its own punishment, paralysis, and bondage. Love says, "Neither do I condemn thee. Go and sin no more." To the mind and heart caught up in the mechanics of fear, this makes little sense, but to the one who is awakening in love, it is clear.

Gandhi is reported to have made the sign of forgiveness to his assassin. In the life and demonstration of this man of love we see the activity of one who was willing to exercise the option of forgiveness. His whole life and its final reported act released a current of love, life, and light that is still operating in the awakening consciousness of mankind.

In the life of Martin Luther King we see the same great activity of love taking place. I know that many who watched and felt the impact of love through him must have sensed, as I am sure he did, the outcome of his special assignment in this particular earthly experience, but he kept on because he had a dream—a dream planted, nourished, and unfolded in him by the universal Creative Spirit of love. His dream, too, as I understand it, is of a humanity freed from fear, punishment, paralysis, and bondage—walking, working, living together in the light of love and freedom.

In a seemingly different field, but clearly related to the awakening of the soul of man, I found evidence of the activity of forgiveness, growth, and freedom in an unusual spot—the Space Center at Huntsville, Alabama. In joyous amazement I looked at the sketches of rockets, energy systems, and other elements of the Space Age as they had come through the mind and heart of a teen-age boy years before man first set foot on the moon. The spirit of love, life, light, and freedom must have whispered to the soul of Werner Von Braun that man is not really an earthbound creature. He is a citizen of the universe destined to explore the fathomless depths of space, both inner and outer. Young Werner Von Braun listened and responded to the voice of the inner spirit. Others listened and responded too, and the Space Age was conceived, born, and launched into the experience of humanity.

Forgiveness, the great option of love, is always open to you and me. Even if our present assignment is not universal in scope, it is part of the universal activity of love, awakening and exercising its option of forgiveness in us, through us, and as us. Thus we are part of the awakening of humanity, part of the ultimate freedom of all mankind, part of the activity of the infinite love that is surely wiping fear, punishment, paralysis, and bondage out of human experience. The age of viciousness is coming to an end in our mind and heart as we exercise the option of forgiveness in the relationships, conditions, and experiences of our daily world.

As a Spiritual Independent, you are always free to exercise the option of forgiveness. Right now you can forgive yourself and others by accepting the forgiving action of infinite love and letting fear, punishment, paralysis, and bondage be wiped out of your past, present, and future. Since you are rapidly becoming a Spiritual Independent, you can decide simply that you are too mature in love and that love is too powerfully at work in you for you to remain the victim of fear, guilt, worry, unforgiveness, punishment, paralysis, bondage. You can watch joyously and gratefully the activity of love at work in you as it cleanses your conscious and subconscious mind of fear and its paralyzing family. You can look at any area or relationship of your life where the elements of fear seem to be operating and say, "I am a Spiritual Independent, and I exercise the option of forgiveness. Infinite Love, forgive us for we know not what we are doing." Instantly you will feel the flow and the activity of love as it responds to your prayer of forgiveness. Remember that God is a God of love, and the justice of that love is always forgiveness, growth, freedom. It is always your privilege to activate and share the option of forgiveness with your world. It is always your privilege to forgive and to be forgiven—to look at every person, relationship, and situation in a dynamic, creative, and adventurous way, and thus to be what you are created to be: a forgiving self-expression of the universal Creative Spirit of love, life, light, and laughter. As love forgives, grows, and sets you free, you will be joining the ranks of an awakening humanity that is moving out of the tunnels of fear into the golden meadows of love.

As you continue to develop your FQ, or forgiveness quotient, you will discover that this option of love is one of the most potent talents that your Creator has given you. A good question to ask yourself several times during each day is this: "Have I been exercising my forgiveness potential to its greatest capacity?" Almost immediately your inner spirit of love, life, light, and laughter will bring to your conscious attention areas of your life, relationships, projects, and conditions where a touch of forgiveness will work miracles. Once we truly become conscious of our FQ we will be as amazed as the followers of Jesus were that "such power had been given unto men." There is no need to further detail the techniques and potentialities of forgiveness, because you will quickly discover them for yourself through actual experience. Forgiveness is the process through which infinite love grows us into the dynamic, creative, adventurous creatures we were designed to be.

As your FQ develops, you may come to the realization that fits into the activity outlined in the following words:

*I am a Spiritual Independent, a creature of love, life, light, and laughter, and I forgive like one. I realize that the power of forgiveness works effectively in every relationship, experience, and area of my life, past, present, and future. I realize that forgiveness is the activity of love in me, through me, and as me, and it gives me the capacity to adopt a healthy, dynamic, creative attitude toward every element of my being and my world.*

## XXIII

# FROM ADULTERY TO ADULTHOOD

By the time most people should have reached adulthood, they have instead entered a state of adultery as the result of their religious, educational, and social training and experience. The root of adultery is idolatry, the false concepts of God and man that have polluted human thought, feeling, and attitudes throughout the centuries. Nowhere in the whole field of human experience are adultery and idolatry more evident than in humanity's sexual experience. One of the most distorted, suppressed, and misunderstood elements of man is his sexual nature. Some try to act as if it doesn't exist; others seem to feel that it must be the work of the devil; others are simply confused by it and are willing to let it go at that. Nonetheless, sex still persists—so as Spiritual Independents we can take a look at it through the clear eyes of love.

A person's attitude toward sex is shaped by his or her consciousness; sexual activity, like every other human interchange, is always a transaction of consciousness. To one in a playboy or playgirl state of consciousness, sex is a plaything; to one in a puritanical, overly moralistic state of consciousness, sex can be a vile, unwelcome, unwholesome thing; to one in a dictatorial, bullying, domineering state of consciousness, sex often becomes a rapacious, crushing, tyrannical thing; to one in a frustrated, unhappy, bitter state of consciousness, sex may well be a frightening, deadly, unsatisfying thing; to one in a lustful, greedy, selfish state of consciousness, sex often appears as an exploitable, cheap, and destructive thing; to a Spiritual Independent, one in whom the spirit of love, life, light, and laughter is awakening, sex (or if you prefer, "sexuality") is becoming a vital, lovely, tender part of all being. Only love, the love that is God, activated in each person, can reveal the true nature of the elements of creation. In love our sexual nature finds its rightful place in the divine plan of beauty, harmony, and life. I am not concerned with the physical equipment and mechanics of sexual activity. There are plenty of "sexperts" in that field, and most of them do a good job of getting their message across. I don't feel impelled to moralize on sex—there are plenty of professionals in that area of human experience, and they have done and are doing competent work. Morality and immorality are elements of that same old coin of conformity or rebellion, and true sexuality, like love, is neither moral nor immoral, it just "is," and I have a feeling that the Spiritual Independent, that awakening creature of love, life, light, and laughter, will find a new and more dynamic and creative way of sexual self-expression than either one. The so-called sexual revolution that has frightened many, delighted many, and no doubt shaken us all to some extent, is evidence that something powerful is going on in this vital area of the human makeup and experience (or shall I call it "sexperience"). As a human being you probably have had, and may still have, your share of sexual taboos, ignorance, and superstition to outgrow. As a Spiritual Independent you are probably by now mature enough to stop conforming to or rebelling against habitual sexual patterns and to take a healthy, dynamic, creative attitude toward every area of your life out of your individual consciousness of love, life, light, and laughter. You are certainly aware that your sexuality has much deeper roots than the physical elements and organs of your being.

One rather unusual attitude toward sex was called to my attention during a lecture in another country. A gentleman got to his feet and started to speak very loudly and with gestures that made me realize he was talking about "sex." My translator managed to convey to me that this man felt, in no uncertain terms, that most of humanity's problems would be solved if only the physical organs of sex could be cut out of men and women and thrown in a great heap and burned. Finally my excited friend

## FROM ADULTERY TO ADULTHOOD

asked me if I agreed with him, and I asked the translator to convey to him that I obviously did not—I had no organs either sexual or otherwise that I cared to contribute to his bonfire. I said if he wanted to get to the real culprits he would have to start with the head and heart of man (and woman, too), and burning them would undoubtedly wreck the rest of the human anatomy. I also pointed out that for years doctors had been removing parts of humanity's sexual equipment without really clearing the sexual picture or the total human picture very much. It is in the adulterous attitudes, the idolatrous concepts that rule the roost in human consciousness, where the problem lies, not in the organs of the body.

If you, as an awakening Spiritual Independent, capable of rising above the opposites of conformity and rebellion in every area of life, are willing to look at the whole sexual scene, and your own sexuality, through the clear eyes of love, life, light, and laughter, you will make some deep, freeing, and refreshing discoveries that will help you to understand and appreciate what is taking place. You will discover that you know many deep and wonderful truths about sex and that you now have the courage to accept and live by them. I have no "new morality" (or immorality), no startling sexual technique to revolutionize your life, no magic pill or potion, no absolute old or new code of ethics to offer, only the suggestion that you stand up on your feet and be a Spiritual Independent, and take a dynamic, creative, and adventurous look at sex.

If you have no problems, opportunities, or interest in this complex field, but have a sure-fire formula that will be of help to others, by all means stop reading and go forth and share the good news with your brothers and sisters who do. There are many who need your love and help because they feel trapped, confused, or frightened in some aspect of the boiling sexual scene, which includes, among other things, traditional marriage and divorce, homosexuality, abortion, pornography, increased crimes against a person such as rape, child abuse, and murder, a loosening of moral taboos and attitudes, the emergence of what would at one time have been startling and shocking patterns in human relationships—and hopefully, a new honesty in looking at the whole scene. Occasionally some viewers threaten the whole scene with hellfire; others proclaim that the solution lies in a return to the good old days and the good old ways. Others seem to feel that the imposition of rigid new laws or the return to old ones is the solution. Others look forward longingly to a heavenly paradise when the trials and tribulations of earthly existence will come to an end; but no doubt most people, and certainly those who are awakening to the spiritual dimensions of their being, feel that the answers must lie in the infinite potentialities of man's awakening spiritual selfhood. There is a song that puts it this way: "Everybody wants to go to heaven, but nobody wants to die!" The threat of hellfire, prohibition, strict laws, rigid patterns of life, or the promise of heavenly paradise, no longer satisfy the awakening spirit in man. There is an inner knowing, a growing realization, which reveals that every element of being, when rightly understood, is pure, beautiful, creative, dynamic, and fulfilling. What we are witnessing and participating in, perhaps reluctantly, is a long-suppressed and overdue sexual revolution that will bring forth a new, healthier, and freer humanity.

In some states of consciousness, there are those who seem to feel that if we dare to look at sex and think about it, we will automatically become sexual athletes, leaping from bed to bed with different partners. But as our understanding of the true nature of sex deepens and expands, through actual experience, we will discover, as my delightful friend Rabbi William Silverman said during a seminar in which we participated, "Man does not live by bed alone!" Sex is not just a pleasant little pastime or game. It is not just the means of procreation and perpetuating the human race. It is not just one of many possible avenues of self-expression. Sex will not go away if we ignore it. It will not disappear if we suppress it. It will not be controlled by outer rules and regulations. It will continue its destructive course if we degrade, debase, or prostitute it. It will reveal its true nature to us

## FROM ADULTERY TO ADULTHOOD

and express its real potential through us only as we assert our spiritual independence and look at it through the clearing eyes of love, life, light, and laughter. You may wish to adopt your own version of the attitude described in the following statements:

*I am a Spiritual Independent, an awakening creature of love, life, light, and laughter, and I look at sex like one. I see sexuality, my own and others, in a new light, the true light of being. I trust my inner knowing that sex, like all the other elements of being, is pure, beautiful, creative, and adventurous. I rejoice as I move out of old states of adultery into a creative fulfilling state of adulthood and maturity.*

Perhaps you are familiar with the greeting card which carries this statement: "Of all my relations I like sex best!" The only thing wrong with this statement, as many ministers, doctors, psychiatrists, bartenders, prostitutes, and other counselors of human beings know full well, is that it is not true for many people. For many men and women, even in this enlightened and free-wheeling age, sex is often a guilt-ridden, tortured, frightening, unhappy, or disappointing experience. What promises to be a dynamic, creative, adventurous experience often turns to ashes in actual practice. The promised ecstasy of the physical sexual act is often blunted by the nagging feeling that something is wrong—that sex is not just what it's supposed to be or what it could be. What's the problem? Why, adultery, of course! What else could it be? And what is adultery? Perhaps outer forms of human behavior first come to mind: wrong people doing wrong things in wrong beds, illicit relationships, illegal acts. But as you know, from actual experience, outer behavior is only the effect of inner attitudes—so acts of adultery stem from adulterous attitudes. Jesus pointed this out when he said that for a man to look at any woman (even his wife!) lustfully is equivalent to the act of committing adultery. And of course, for a woman to look at any man (even her husband) lustfully would have the same effect. Just to legalize or institutionalize an adulterous act does not make it right, loving, or moral. Then what happens when a man looks at a woman lustfully? He becomes a victim of adultery. Certainly lust involves more than the desire to take a woman to bed, to engage physically in the act of sexual intercourse. Is it not also to transgress her integrity as a person, to think of her and to treat her as a pawn, an object, a body into which he can pour his passion or empty his frustrations, violence, and failures? Is it not to treat her as an inferior creature or as an attractive and useful bit of furniture and to ignore her real identity as a spiritual being, a daughter of the Infinite, a free, beautiful, and inviolable person? Is it not to invade and violate the sacred temple of her personality and body in thought, feeling, and attitude? Is it not to be unloving, untrue, disloyal to the radiant, free spirit and person of them both? (And what is adultery for a man is also adultery for a woman.) Marriage rarely heals such an attitude of adultery—it often merely legalizes and institutionalizes it. Ministers, doctors, psychiatrists, and other counselors often hear wives complain that their husbands don't really love them. They ignore them unless the husbands are sexually aroused, they treat them like beautiful and useful pieces of furniture, they buy them expensive gifts and gadgets but ignore them as women and as persons. If they are attractive women, their husbands may enjoy showing them off to company and then cut them down and keep them "in their place" in private. Some wives will go so far as to say that they feel like well-paid, beautifully dressed, lavishly housed prostitutes. Husbands often complain, too, that their wives ignore them as men, as persons, that they consider their husbands "a good catch" or think of them as a meal ticket or a source of supply, have little or only a feigned interest in sexual relations, and seem to feel that, since everything is legal, anything goes! Men and women caught up in this type of marriage relationship are the victims of adultery even if the marriage has been legalized and institutionalized in a beautiful ceremony by a Catholic pope, a Protestant bishop, a Jewish rabbi, or any other official authorized by society to perform that function.

While we are at it, we might just as well take a look at what has become almost a corollary to marriage: divorce. Divorce, as it is usually practiced, is a natural outgrowth of adulterous marriage. Divorce is rarely much better than the marriage it seemingly terminates, because the participants often continue in their states of adultery, merely moving on to inflict them on other partners. As in the days of the horse and carriage, the leading cause of divorce is marriage—not marriage as an ideal relationship, but marriage as it is so often practiced in states of adultery. Jesus pointed out that divorce can cause both marriage partners to commit adultery. Another way of looking at it is that when a marriage begins to come apart at the seams, the adulterous glue that held it together becomes apparent. It is often discovered that the attraction that supposedly brought the couple together was really fear masquerading as love rather than love itself. To enter into a true state of marriage, a man and woman need to leave their father and mother and cleave to each other, that is, begin a new life based on the integrity of their own souls and the challenge, inspiration, and adventure of a truly new and unique relationship. Unfortunately, what happens so often is that the newlyweds find that they have taken mama's and papa's hangups and adulterous attitudes right along with them and have even added something from grandma and grandpa, and that organized religion, society, and education have also added their quota of adulterous attitudes.

Often counselors who are trying to prevent the breakup of a marriage and infuse new life into it, hear complaints like this from the threatened wife: "I just don't understand why my husband is leaving me for that young hussy. I always let him have sex as often as he wanted it." One is sometimes tempted to ask whether the husband was required to give written notice of his desire for sex or if verbal requests were sufficient. Sometimes it is the bewildered husband who laments: "I just can't understand why she doesn't love me any more. I've always treated her right. I gave her a beautiful home, her own car, I always remembered our anniversaries, gave her all the sex she could take—and now she is leaving me."

At other times an offended husband or wife will complain: "I gave everything I had to our marriage and I can't understand where I've failed. My marriage has always been the most important thing in my life to me. I would give anything to preserve it." Those statements may be accurate, but basically the attitudes they reveal are adulterous. The marriage was the most important thing in the life of the individual concerned, probably for a variety of reasons. It represented security, prestige, accomplishment, or some other value. The marriage was much more important than the mate as a person, as an individual, as a growing, unfolding creature of love, life, light, and laughter. The marriage was even more important than the individual to whom it was the most important—so naturally the marriage failed, or at least it began to come apart because no marriage (or any other human relationship for that matter) is strong enough and important enough to be an end in itself. Marriage, like the sabbath, was made for man and woman, not the other way around.

Jesus pointed out that there is a state of awareness in which people no longer marry or are given in marriage.

"People in this world," Jesus replied, "marry and are given in marriage. But those who are considered worthy of reaching that world, which means rising from the dead, neither marry nor are they given in marriage. They cannot die any more but live like the angels; for being children of the resurrection, they are the sons of God."

While total resurrection from the dead concepts of the past may be some time away, there is no denying that there are revolutionary changes in the marriage picture since Jesus' day—and undoubtedly, there are more to come. There are no longer the social, religious, economic, or other pressures to hold a marriage together. Both men and women are freer, more conscious of their worth as persons, and less willing than ever before to continue an adulterous, stagnating, or dead relationship. (While we are primarily concerned here with marriage and divorce, you will readily see that most of the principles involved apply in the whole field of human relationships.) Often, individuals who continue to live together in a nominal marriage are really living in a state of divorce—they just haven't legalized it.

## FROM ADULTERY TO ADULTHOOD

A vital, creative, adventurous marriage relationship requires more from the marriage partners today than ever before. Marriage is not an automatic, binding, self-perpetuating relationship any longer—if it ever was. The life, vitality, and strength of a marriage relationship must come through both of the partners. Society, religion, or other institutions can't guarantee the success of a marriage. Like every other creative, adventurous, fulfilling relationship, marriage is alive only when the mighty L-current of love, life, light, and laughter finds ever greater expression in it. The marriage license is not a bill of sale or certificate of title. It does not authorize one person to dominate, submerge, bind, or drain another. It provides a legal and social base on which a man and a woman (and others as well, particularly where children are involved) are free to establish an atmosphere of love in which everyone involved can grow and unfold his or her spiritual potential. While persons in a marriage (and in other relationships as well) may belong with each other for reasons of growth and unfoldment, they do not really belong to each other.

As a Spiritual Independent, what do you think Jesus had in mind when he spoke of the state of awareness in which people no longer marry or are given in marriage? You are entitled to your own thoughts and feelings, insights, and intuitions. It seems to me that he was pointing out the growth in levels of consciousness. These states of consciousness always have to do with our relationship with the Creator as well as with each other. We go through all kinds of relationships in our search for the ultimate relationship, oneness—oneness with God and oneness with each other. We speak of the marriage of the human self to the divine self, of man to God, of each one to the Christ within. These are preliminary states culminating in the highest state of all, the state of total unity or oneness, which Jesus described in the words, "I and the Father are one." Once we come into that realization, then all the preliminary relationships have come to an end. This changes everything in our relationship with our Creator. We realize that we are a self-expression of the infinite source, the Creative Spirit of love, life, light, and laughter, and we no longer have to go through so many complicated rituals, covenants, and relationships.

We also go through similar experiences in our relationships with each other. Eventually we will realize that, as we are one with our Creator, we are also one with our neighbor. We might put it in words like this: *"I realize that I am one with my Creator—and I realize that I and my neighbor are one also."*

When this realization really takes over in us, all our old attempts to establish oneness through covenants, contracts, possessiveness, and other outer forms of attachment are over. This is certainly going to have a profound impact on the institution of marriage, as well as friendships and other relationships. The future of all human relationships, including marriage, lies ultimately not in outer rules and regulations, covenants, or contracts, but in the unfolding spiritual nature of men and women. When the mighty L-current has wiped fear, ignorance, insecurity, and superstition out of human minds and hearts, the new creatures that men and women become will establish a different order in all relationships.

It seems doubtful that divorce ever really brings a relationship to an end—not even death can do that! A relationship as intimate as marriage, particularly where children are involved, has deep roots. A legal document of separation or divorce doesn't guarantee anything more than the marriage license did. We are all vital, creative, spiritual beings, and legalizing or institutionalizing our relationships is only a surface attempt to deal with elements of being that lie within our inner nature. The more intimately we become acquainted with the depths of our being, the more capable we are of enriching all of our relationships. Becoming conscious of our inner spirit of love, life, light, and laughter changes our contribution to and participation in marriage, divorce, family, friendship, and every other type of human association.

Sometimes I am asked if I am in favor of divorce and I say honestly, "No, at least not the usual kind—but, for that matter, neither am I in favor of marriage as it is so often practiced. What I really desire for all human beings are dynamic, creative, adventurous, fulfilling relationships—relationships that stir people, inspire them, and help to make them conscious of what they really are. It would be wonderful if all marriages were of that nature."

So, if you are involved in or contemplating marriage, divorce, family, friendship, or any other relationship that the fertile mind and heart of humanity can conceive, remember who and what you are, a Spiritual Independent, and act accordingly. Be loyal to the royal spirit of the Infinite that is within, rather than to institution, dogma, or outer pressure. Remember that you are love, you live in love, that you are a creature of love, life, light, and laughter. If you become aware that you are being victimized by a state of adultery, do something about it. Stand up on your spiritual feet and move lovingly and confidently from adultery to adulthood. You are learning, from actual experience, to do that more joyously all the time.

# XXIV

# LOVE AND COSMIC SEXUALITY

(What you have always known about sex and are now ready to accept)

Fear makes adulterers, idolaters, and cowards out of all in whom it operates. Anyone who is victimized by fear is living in a tight little corner of his individual potential, aware of and exercising only a tiny band of the powerful current of creative energy (the L-current) available to him. Men and women, created to be cosmic creatures, often poke along in stagnant, inadequate, unproductive relationships and activities, trapped by fear, habit, and inertia. Hopefully, however, the chain of limitation is being broken, and both women and men are entering the experience of liberation. The man/woman relationship is the most important in humanity, and true freedom will come only when both sexes have accepted and are expressing their true nature. In spite of the turmoil and confusion, our vision is clearing, and we can catch at least a glimpse of the picture described in the following words:

> I have seen the free-born woman
> Standing side by side with man.
> I have seen the nations broaden
> Till there is no tribe or clan,
> And the war-lords all have vanished
> In the love of man for man.
> God's truth is marching on.
>
> Henry Victor Morgan

## LOVE AND COSMIC SEXUALITY

As we move from the old adulterous states that have bound humanity for so long and approach adulthood, we enter a state of spiritual independence where we have the courage to take a loving, dynamic, and creative look at our own sexuality. It is difficult to describe this state of spiritual independence. We are either in it or we are not. It reminds me of the story told about the late jazz master Louis Armstrong. A young man who was considered to be a very promising jazz musician somehow got an appointment with Satchmo. The first question the brash youngster asked after he was introduced was: "Just what is jazz, Mr. Armstrong?" In my imagination, I can just see those bright eyes and sparkling smile flash as the Maestro answered: "Man, ya gotta ask—ya ain't got it!"

Love brings us to that point in our own unfoldment where we realize we can trust our own consciousness and look at ourself fearlessly and joyously. Either we have reached the state of being a Spiritual Independent or we have not. If we are a Spiritual Independent, we can look at our sexuality in love and let it unfold its attitudes, desires, energies, functions, and relationships. If we are not spiritually independent, we can go back to following the best rules and regulations that are available. For a little practice, we can take ideas like those contained in the following words into our inner being and see what happens:

*I am a Spiritual Independent, a cosmic human being, and I have the sexual attitudes, desires, energies, functions, and relationships of one. I am letting the sexual elements of being unfold in me in love.*

As the process these words describe unfolds you, you may discover that your understanding of sex and sexuality has been pretty narrow and constricted. Sexuality has spiritual as well as mental, emotional, and physical dimensions. And you will discover that your masculinity or your femininity, as the gender may be, is in reality your divinity. When the Creative Spirit of love, life, light, and laughter makes man in its image, *they* come out male and female.

"So God created man in His own image, in the image of God created He him; male and female created He them."

This discovery will come as no surprise to you. You will realize that deep down within, you have known it all along; but now you are spiritually mature enough to accept it. In fact, this discovery may come as a considerable relief to you because it is quite possible that sex, in the conventional sense—with its conventional taboos, conventional relationships, conventional activities, whether rated as moral or immoral—had just about run its course in your experience. You realize that the day-to-day variety of sex, which was so often condemned, moralized, commercialized, exploited, bought and sold, bartered, mechanized, advertised, played with, was pretty much a surface thing, and you had reached a point where you could take it or leave it. It may have been pleasant and habitual, but something deep within you yearned for deeper, more creative and adventurous self-expression. No doubt you had accepted sex as an important element in the procreation, reproduction, and perpetuation of the human race, with some plus benefits along the way, but hadn't really given it much acceptance as a vital part of your spiritual nature and unfoldment. Perhaps you had even decided that you had risen above sex and were able to give it up, with a feeling of release from the sexual antics of the human scene.

Now you can, if you choose, look at sexuality, your own and others, with cosmic vision, through the eyes of a Spiritual Independent. You can move from outer manifestations of sexuality, its physical organs and functions, through the mental concepts and emotional attachments to it, to the inner dimensions of the spiritual reality. The process is no longer strange to you, if it ever was, because it is the way you have discovered that you are a creature of love, life, light, and laughter. Now you can recognize (re-cognize, or re-know) what you have always known deep within your being, that you are male or female, a vital part of the "image of God," a masculine or feminine self-expression of the Divine Ego. It is interesting and inspiring to realize that the image of God is male and female because it confirms a great truth that you have always known: male and female are not two *opposite* sexes—rather, they are complementary elements in the one sexuality, and they stimulate, inspire, and complete each other, as a radiant, beautiful, harmonious self-expression of the Infinite. "The battle of the sexes" has largely been based on the false assumption, belief, and feeling that there are *two* sexes in the universe, and that they are opposed to each other. Just as there is only one God, one Love, one Life, one Self, there is only one sex (or sexuality), with complementary male and female elements. Of course, you have always known this at physical levels. Even a superficial acquaintance with the physical bodies of men and women gets the message across. And if you have engaged in the physical act of sexual intercourse with a member of the complementary sex, whatever joy, beauty, satisfaction, and sense of wonder you experienced in it revealed the oneness of sexuality and some degree of the power and glory of uniting its male and female elements. Also, in a relatively negative sense, your growing disenchantment with some of the less-than-fulfilling attitudes, activities, and relationships involving men and women reveals your innate knowledge that sexual relationships should be beautiful, pure, and good.

Male and female elements operate throughout all creation. They are present in atoms, molecules, plants, animals, thoughts, feelings, conscious and subconscious mind, spirit and matter, electromagnetic fields—in all areas of being. Both of these elements are present in you, in the atoms and cells of your body, in the functions of your mind and your emotions, in the relationships between your spiritual and other elements, in the relationship between you and God. Some think of God as Father; others worship God as the Great Mother; others think of Father-Mother God. Marriage, divorce, adultery, and other sexual relationships and activities also have their function in our consciousness. We might think of the ideal marriage in terms of consciousness, as the harmonious functioning of the conscious and subconscious mind, the union of all the other elements of your being with the Christ nature in you, the union or the communion of your soul with God. Divorce in terms of consciousness comes about when old states of mind and heart are outgrown, when they die, when they are given up for something higher and better. Adultery takes place when we feed our inner and outer systems of self-realization and expression with fearful and false concepts, erroneous beliefs, and adulterated views of reality. In its deepest, truest, and most radiant sense, this is a sexual universe, and you are a cosmic being through whom its sexual elements are to find free and creative intercourse and expression on all levels and in all relationships. Of course, to comprehend this, one has to expand his awareness and understanding of what sex is—but isn't this true of any area of being? We can never know the truth of anything until and unless we are willing to release our tight little opinions of it. We tend to live in a labelistic world. Often, rather than do our own thinking and feeling, we accept words as labels and just assume that that's all there is to it. This is particularly true in the areas of sex and sexuality. Just the words "sex" or "adultery" or "marriage" or "divorce" are enough to trigger all kinds of tight little pictures in some states of consciousness. You, as a Spiritual Independent, however, have outgrown the labelistic approach to life. You have the courage, confidence, and will to look at everything in a new light, and as you do this, you discover all kinds of dimensions in what had formerly appeared like tight little boxes.

The writers of the Bible were no strangers to the true nature of the universe and its creatures and its Creator. In fact, the Bible is the most fantastic manual on sexuality that there is. It contains the whole story, from the spiritual nature of cosmic sexuality through all the relationships—marriage, divorce, adultery; the bondage of men and women in the dark night of fear, ignorance, and superstition; and the truth that sets men and women free.

You have always known (this knowledge has been imprinted in the very atoms and cells of your being) that your sexuality is holy, pure, and sacred. You have always known that it was not to be exploited, suppressed, adulterated, distorted, cheapened, degraded, prostituted—and when you have engaged in activities or relationships that were out of tune with your true sexual nature, you have felt uncomfortable, cheated, frustrated, disgusted, trapped, or in bondage of some kind.

## LOVE AND COSMIC SEXUALITY

Now, as an awakening creature of love, life, light, and laughter, you can accept your cosmic sexuality, your masculinity or your femininity, as a vital part of the image of God, the divinity that you are. Probably just reading these words is releasing a current of energy that makes you feel freer in heart, soul, mind, and body. Old congestions, hangups, fears, guilts, inertias are miraculously letting go. Waves of understanding and currents of new life energy are flowing through your entire being from the inner spiritual depths to the atoms, cells, and organs of your body. Your whole being is freed from any false and limiting concepts you have entertained in it. A wonderful sense of purity, cleansing, and renewal is spreading throughout you. A process which a friend of mine describes as "virgintensification" is taking place. You are being resurrected from the dead ruts of mortal sense. Sometimes the powerful currents of energy may seem almost exquisitely unbearable because their intensity and vibrations are so high. Do not be concerned; even these intense currents of energy are but forerunners of greater ones to come, as elements of your being are awakened to their true potential.

If you are a woman you may wish to meditate occasionally on ideas such as those contained in the following words:

*I am a Spiritual Independent, a woman, a cosmic female, a daughter of the Infinite. My femininity is my divinity. My person, from its innermost spiritual depths to the organs of my body, is a holy, pure, sacred temple of the infinite Creative Spirit. I respect the integrity of my own being. I extend that respect to the members of my sex and to the members of the complementary sex.*

If you are a man you can easily revise that meditation accordingly.

You will almost immediately become aware of the activity that these words describe and indicate. This activity is a self-unfoldment process that has undoubtedly been delayed and suppressed for a long time. While most of humanity has been asleep to its real identity and potential, now at last we are being awakened and helping to accelerate that awakening process. I think you will enjoy a little item that someone sent me. I don't know where it came from, but here it is:

## ALMOST EVERYBODY AT SOME TIME HAS SAID SOMETHING WONDERFUL

> The Buddha, for instance:
> who, when reverently asked
> by his followers
> > if he were a god,
> > > an angel, a saint,
> three times responded
> with a simple "no."
>
> "Then what are you?"
> "I am awake," he said.

You are awake, and you will be awakened even more completely by that mighty L-current of love, life, light, and laughter that is now unfolding your true sexuality, your masculinity or your femininity. You will find that some remarkable changes are taking place in your attitudes toward yourself and toward others, and in your relationships. To look at a boy and realize that his boyhood is his divinity; or at a girl and realize that her girlhood is her divinity; or at a man and realize that his masculinity is his divinity; or at a woman and realize that her femininity is her divinity, works an almost instant change for the better in your relationship with that person. It also brings a new dimension to the reality and immanence of the image of God in your neighbor and in yourself. I know there are those who claim that eventually we will reach a state of sexlessness, but I haven't seen any indication that the sexual nature of creation is about to be repealed. It is our inadequate concept of sex that is going to be eliminated. In any event, we might just as well learn to enjoy and appreciate what we have now so that we will be ready for whatever is to come.

As we love and appreciate our cosmic sexuality, it will grow

## LOVE AND COSMIC SEXUALITY

and unfold in wonderful ways, and we will discover in increasing measure what it means to be a man or a woman created in the image and after the likeness of God, the universal Creative Spirit of love, life, light, and laughter. As we move and are moved from old stereotypes of sexuality to its cosmic dimensions, we will find that we are entering a new way of life in which we don't have to fight quite so hard for what belongs to us. As a woman once said to me: "I am so busy exercising the privileges of being a woman that I don't have time to worry about my rights."

Fear in one form or another is always concerned about its rights. Love is busy exercising its privileges. Both women and men need liberation, and that liberation will come quickly as they exercise their privileges and potentialities.

You might want to think about it this way:

*I am a Spiritual Independent, a cosmic creature, and I am so busy exercising the privileges of my true nature that my rights take care of themselves.*

There is no need for me to try to outline the privileges of being a man or a woman conscious of cosmic sexuality. You are discovering and exercising these in your own inimitable, refreshing, and fulfilling way. You are realizing that your attitudes toward yourself, members of your own sex, and members of the complementary sex are constantly being improved, lifted up, and freed. Something wonderful has been released within you—your sexuality, your selfhood—and it is constantly revealing new and more creative and adventurous ways to love and live and shine and laugh and enjoy this adventure in growth that we all share. If you are a man you may find that your attitudes toward specific women are changing, but so also is your attitude toward all women. You may even, in your secret heart of hearts, forgive yourself for the ignorant attitudes you have inflicted upon the women in your life, and enter with me into a prayer of gratitude which I have entitled "Adam Thanks You":

> Oh, Woman, Sweet, Beautiful Eve—
> Cosmic female that you are . . .
> Glad am I

## HOW TO LOVE YOUR NEIGHBOR

That you came down from your star
In the sky
To don the lovely garments of flesh
To probe the mystery and ecstasy of life
And to refresh
And walk the earth with me.

If you are a woman and share a similar feeling and attitude toward men, you can either rephrase the words or, from that beautiful, cosmic female heart of yours, pour out a current of love and gratitude with or without words.

Once again, of course, we are confronted with the delightful, challenging, and inspiring assignment of living in the earth that which we are discovering to be true in heaven. To be a cosmic male or female in the secret place of our inner being is one thing; to live it in our very demanding, down-to-earth relationships is another phase of the dramatic creative adventure. But for yet a little while, let us continue the inner vision. Can you see and feel what a paradise it will be when humanity has discovered its cosmic identity, its spiritual reality? when men and women will no longer be afraid or guilty or ashamed or embarrassed or possessive or insecure? when there is no longer any death—and therefore no longer any birth? Can you imagine what it will be like when men and women look at each other through pure eyes—and feel each other through the pure heart of love and life and light and laughter? Can you catch the vision of a race of beings in which each one is loyal to the royal within the other? Can you foretell the future of institutions and activities like the church, marriage, divorce, sexual intercourse, and other human relationships, when each individual is free in the knowledge of his own divinity and that of his neighbor? These are not idle dreams but are quite within the reach and experience of awakening human potential.

But now we must be practical and take the inner vision, the inner scene, and the inner feeling into the relationships of our very "practical" earth. Move into your marriage or your divorce or your engagement or your friendship or your family or your office, or any other place or activity where cosmic human beings become involved with each other, carrying the awareness of your own cosmic sexuality and that of all others with you. It is easy to predict that changes will take place in both your inner and outer world. Some relationships will be revitalized, brought into creative, adventurous activity. Some will be expanded, perhaps even to the point where, in an outer sense, they seem to be terminated because they have fulfilled their purpose. It is well to remember that love not only brings together and maintains relationships, it also expands them, fulfills them, and of course terminates them when one (or more) of the individuals involved really needs to move on for the benefit of all concerned. You are coming alive in love, you are becoming conscious of your own person, your own selfhood, your own sexuality, and you will play an ever more creative role in any relationship of which you are a part. Whatever you are called upon to do, you will do in love in a lively, radiant, joyous way because that is what you are becoming, a cosmic creature of love, life, light, and laughter.

Married or unmarried, divorced or undivorced, man or woman of the world, or even celibate, you are discovering more of the cosmic energies and dimensions of your own divine sexuality, and you will be less and less afraid to express it, to share it, to respect it—and to love and appreciate that divinity within others in your life.

You will know that there is a constant communication and intercourse going on between you and all others at many different levels. If you enter into the physical act of sexual intercourse with a member of the complementary sex, you will realize that it is no longer just a physical act, just a release of passion, but that it is indeed a holy sacrament, shared by two children of the Infinite, and that at least one of them is conscious of what is taking place. If it is for the purpose of procreation—what could be holier and more sacred than the inner and outer preparation of a body through which another living soul will incarnate for an earthly experience. Every soul incarnating for an earthly experience yearns to do so through a holy, pure, sacred act of love by its human parents. If it is part of a spontaneous, creative, fulfilling relationship arranged by love itself for another of its own high purposes, it is still holy, pure, and sacred, for by now you will see and feel that:

> Every Adam is a living universe
> and so is every Eve—
> And when they meet
>     to deeply unite
>     in love and freedom
>     another bright
>     new universe is born
>     and whether or not
>     this universe of throbbing light
>     is clothed in flesh
>     to walk the earth in human form,
>     broken is the norm—
>     and the world is never quite so dark again.
>
>                          (*Poetic License*)

If you are reminded that liberty is not license, agree gently, oh, so gently, remembering that it is not up to the wiggling, cocooned worm to legislate the activity and feeling of the winged butterfly, nor is it the prerogative of the scratching, dust-scratching chickens to dictate the flight of the eagle. Remember also that it is not the business of the butterfly to kick apart the cocoon from which it so recently emerged, nor is it rewarding for the eagle to try to wreck chicken yards. Neither the butterfly nor the eagle are truly free unless and until they are willing to *let* the light and inspiration of their flight inspire others. The cocoons will dissolve after they have served their purpose. The chicken yards will be emptied as the growing light of freedom dawns in more and more of awakening humanity. It is well to remember, too, that sometimes we may think we have the wings of a butterfly and of an eagle when we have only looked through a pinhole in the cocoon into the flyable sky or are still sitting on the fence listening to the persuaders who urge us to surge up into the blue. We are dealing with a new dimension of freedom. This liberty is not license—the license of conformity, those permits issued by society, authorizing its members to practice marriage, divorce, religion, medicine, law, war, or peace on each other; nor is it the license of rebellion that flaunts established methods or "kicks over the traces" merely as a show of independence. We are experiencing the liberty, the glorious liberty of the awakening sons and daughters of the Infinite, and all of our relations with all of our neighbors are prompted and fulfilled from deep levels of being—the center of love, life, light, and laughter within us all.

Is this free love—indiscriminate, promiscuous sex? With a deep inner chuckle, you know, feel, and see more clearly than that. You are discovering that love is not "free." Love is the most unique, dynamic, creative, and adventurous discipline and energy in the universe. Love is not indiscriminate, promiscuous, adulterous in any of its relationships and activities. Love awakens us and moves us inevitably and irresistibly out of the old stereotypes of men and women, personality and sexuality, into a growing realization of our own cosmic identity and nature. Step by step, event by event, relationship by relationship, experience by experience, we are discovering what it is to be a real person. We are learning, in love, to give life, light, joy, loyalty, and liberty to the reality that we are. We are learning to love our neighbor as ourself, to recognize, accept, love, and respect the real person that he or she is, and to let love dissolve forever the old, fearful, adulterous, binding attitudes that have kept human beings from becoming the cosmic creatures that they are.

We are witnessing and taking part in a spiritual, social, and sexual revolution that is bringing forth a new pattern in human experience and relationship—a pattern no longer imposed by outer pressures but unfolded from within and through each person as the cosmic L-current of love, life, light, and laughter awakens its sons and daughters to the infinite dimensions of their own cosmic sexuality.

The real person awakening in each one of us cannot be confined to the mental, emotional, economic, social, religious, or other structures that have evolved through the centuries. A new order is being brought forth from the deep, eternal, infinite center of each person. Eventually each man will know what a real man is, each woman will know what a real woman is, and they will share their growing awareness in dynamic, creative, and adventurous relationships that are as far removed from the old conformity/rebellion patterns of the past as the flight of the eagle is removed from the scratching of chickens in the dust.

No doubt, more often than ever before you will turn to the universal Creative Spirit of love, life, light, and laughter either in silent communion or with words, thoughts, and feelings:
*Infinite Creative Spirit of love, open my whole being ever wider to the mighty L-current of love, life, light, and laughter. I rejoice in my own awakening selfhood. I accept my cosmic sexuality. I love it. I respect it. I am loyal to it. I accept the cosmic sexuality of every person in my world. I love it. I respect it. I am loyal to it. Let every man in my life feel my love, my acceptance, my respect, my loyalty, and through that feeling be more of the real man you created him to be. Let every woman in my life feel my love, my acceptance, my respect, my loyalty, and through that feeling be more of the woman you created her to be. Let all of our relationships be holy, pure, and sacred—loving, alive, radiant, joyous as we move out of the ruts of conformity and rebellion into the glorious liberty of the sons and daughters of the living God of love.*

You are no stranger to yourself. In your deep center of being you have always known who and what you are. Now you are accepting, becoming, and being what you have always known. You are a living, vital part of the pure vision that is awakening in us all:

What is pure? Who is pure?—I asked—and I felt the whole universe prepare to answer. As I waited in grateful amazement,

## LOVE AND COSMIC SEXUALITY

the inner and outer smog cleared and I saw and heard all creation and every creature shining and singing "I Am—I Am—I Am!" Behind and in and through all that is, I beheld the pure Spirit of Creation at work directing the pure current of love, life, and light into pure form and activity.

Then I caught a glimpse of the purity of my Self. I saw and felt the pure current of love, life, and light individualizing me, pouring into my heart as pure feeling, into my soul as pure form, through my lips as pure words, into my world as pure action, and through my eyes as pure seeing. I heard the song of the pure "I Am" of being in me.

Then I saw, felt, and heard pure humanity—shining, loving, singing—"I Am—I Am—I Am!" I watched the pure current of love, life, and light—the creative word of the Infinite One becoming flesh and being my technicolor neighbors—flowing into self-expression in, through, and as each one. And we looked at each other through pure hearts, souls, minds, and eyes—and we saw each other as pure as the Creator.

Then I asked an ignorant question: "Where is all the seeming impurity?" There was none to answer—but the smog returned quickly, stinging my eyes, my heart, my soul, my mind—

All of which leads me to realize that Creator and Creation are pure—but it takes pure vision to see and feel that purity. On a flight from Jamaica to New York City, I had a most interesting lesson in the importance of vision. As I looked at the beautiful cloud formations over the water I became aware that there was a flaw in the window through which I was looking. There was a little blemish in the glass, and as I tried to look through that blemish at the beautiful scene I found that it was completely distorted and thrown out of focus. Nothing had happened to the scenery that I was viewing. It was merely that the window through which I was looking had a flaw in it. When our vision is distorted by fear, ignorance, selfishness, or condemnation, it seems that everything we see is distorted, out of focus, wrong, but when the mighty L-current of love, life, light, and laughter clears up our vision we enter a new world, the real world that has always been. Practice seeing yourself, your neighbor, sex, life, and all its relationships through the pure vision of love, and rejoice as the distorted pictures in the cracked old mirror of human consciousness disappear. Be what you are—a cosmic creature created in the image of the Infinite Spirit of love, life, light, and laughter.

## XXV

## THE LASER BEAM OF SPIRIT

This is going to be a short chapter, but it carries a big proposal. I invite you to build a laser beam of spiritual energy which will help you to accelerate the freeing process that is awakening humanity to its infinite potential as the family of love, life, light, and laughter. Our scientists are delighted with the discovery of the laser—an acronym for Light Amplification by Stimulated Emission of Radiation. As I understand it, a laser beam of light differs from ordinary light sources in purity and directionality.

> While ordinary light is composed of a vast array of colors (or as physicists say, electromagnetic frequencies), laser light is composed of only one frequency. Furthermore, while light waves in ordinary light proceed outward from their source—a light bulb for example—in random order, light waves from a laser are all co-ordinated in time and space. As a consequence, laser light can be precisely controlled and focused. In tests to check the diffusion of laser light, a beam from a ruby laser was aimed at the moon, 240,000 miles away. When it reached the lunar surface the beam covered an area approximately two miles in diameter. A beam from a searchlight, however, would spread out to cover an area tens of thousands of miles across. Considered from a different perspective, laser beams can be focused to a point a single wavelength in diameter, thus concentrating the beam's energy on an unbelievably small area.

Now I am proposing that we set out to develop a laser beam of spiritual energy that will operate in the mental and emotional fields of human consciousness. As a start I suggest that we use a new set of words as a source for "laser": "Love Activated Spiritual Energy Ray." You are already discovering the intensified flow of love, life, light, and laughter into self-expression through you. I know from my own experience, and experiences shared by others, that this mighty L-current can be focused into a "love activated spiritual energy ray" that has the capacity to work in human consciousness to help wipe out fear, guilt, ignorance, superstition, and all the other elements of darkness that still bind and suppress human potential. Love gives us the opportunity to overcome the problems of humanity in our own consciousness, but it also expands that opportunity and lets us work to help others. I am convinced that when Jesus said, "Let your light shine," he was not just talking about a general, happy type of radiation. He was being very specific about a potent ray of love, life, and light that each one who follows him in seeking the kingdom, finding it, and expressing it, will discover.

Teilhard de Chardin, the noted Jesuit priest-scientist, suggests that a new envelope of consciousness, that is, thought and feeling, is being formed in the atmosphere around the earth. Each one who is awakening to his potential as a creature of love, life, light, and laughter has the capacity to add to the potency and power of this developing envelope that is even now encircling the earth. We are not helpless in the face of problems that seem to be threatening humanity today. When we become aware of a crisis in human experience, we do not have to retreat into our spiritual storm cellars. Instead, we can consciously direct a "love activated spiritual energy ray" of healing, freeing power, not at individuals or outer circumstances but into the deep inner recesses of human consciousness where fear, guilt, and ignorance still hang on. St. Paul pointed out that our real enemies lie not in outer circumstance or person but in the dark principalities of man's inner consciousness. Jesus also pointed out that the enemies we have to overcome are not people but the "enemies of our own household," those inner states of fear, ignorance, and superstition that keep us less than we truly are.

We will be working together in a new field, but one in which we are no longer strangers. You have been experiencing the flow of energy from the deep center within yourself, that mighty L-current of love, life, light, and laughter that is renewing your mind, refreshing and refleshing your body, transforming your relationships, and, above all, bringing you to a deeper realization of your true selfhood. I am urging you to take the knowledge that you have gained through actual self-experience to begin to concentrate this increased energy flow that is moving through you into a laser beam of love, life, and light that you can direct to any place in human consciousness where it is needed. I need not tell you the where and the how of this activity, because you are conscious of your own selfhood. You are open to the guidance and the creative energy of the universal Creative Spirit, and if you need guidance you know where and how to ask for it. I cannot impress upon you too greatly the fantastic significance of what you will be doing.

Man has probably reached this point of unfoldment before. He has undoubtedly discovered atomic energy before. He has perhaps even unlocked some of the great secrets of mind and spirit before, and he has probably blown up whole civilizations before. But I feel that this time the outcome will be different, because there are enough people like you who are becoming conscious of their cosmic being, their reality, their selfhood, and who are willing to lay hold of this dynamic and creative current of living energy to become, as St. Paul puts it, "co-creators with God."

We are not playing a game of marbles or tiddlywinks. We are not caught up in an activity that appeals to idolaters, adulterers, or cowards. We are invited to step into the stream of human evolution and become part of its cutting edge. In the experiences shared in this book, we have become acquainted with our selfhood, our cosmic sexuality, our life-giving spirit. We are prepared, or will shortly be prepared, to spread our wings and soar into the flyable skies of our new selfhood. We will be expanding old relationships, discovering new dimensions in present activities, moving out of other relationships, discovering new companions, entering new, creative, and adventurous relationships that could not even have occurred to us before. We will no longer be so tightly bound by the mental and emotional hitching posts of our past. We may touch wing tips, mind tips, heart tips, or we may become deeply involved in special projects and each other—but we will know and be known by each other. Our mutual recognition will be instant, deep, and powerful. We will feel the increasing intensity of the L-current as it flows to us and through us and between us into the world. As we love and respect and salute each other, new worlds of light will come into being, and they will be added to the growing envelope of love, life, light, and laughter that is already embracing the world. One of these days, and it may be much closer than we consciously realize, the scale of consciousness will be tipped, and fear, darkness, and ignorance will no longer hold sway in the minds and hearts of men.

Take the time, whenever you can make or accept the opportunity, to exercise your growing ability to concentrate and focus the energy flowing through you into a "love activated spiritual energy ray" that, linked with others, becomes a mighty stream of irresistible light. Thank you for joining me in this incredibly rich, fantastically adventurous, gloriously freeing experience of loving your neighbor as yourself. If and whenever we meet in person, that will be the occasion for a celebration of love, life, light, and laughter. If our personal meeting is delayed, our souls have touched in love, and through that contact we are both freer, stronger, and more alive. Over the invisible ribbons of love that link us, my joy and gratitude flow to you in ever-growing measure. It's great to be alive in love and to discover that we have been there all the time!

# XXVI

# REMINDERS

This chapter contains a number of ideas which I feel you will wish to consider and expand in your own mind, heart, and life. Many of the selections are from the Bible and I have used the Phillips translation because of its simplicity and clarity. Whenever you feel the need for a reminder, you may wish to refer to this chapter and pick out an idea or two to refresh your consciousness.

"You shall not seek revenge, or cherish anger towards your kinsfolk; you shall love your neighbor as a man like yourself. I am the Lord" (Leviticus 19:18).

"O, Israel, listen: Jehovah is our God, Jehovah alone. You must love him with all your heart, soul, and might. And you must think constantly about these commandments I am giving you today" (Deuteronomy 6:5).

"And one of the scribes came up and heard them disputing with one another, and seeing that he answered them well, asked him, 'Which commandment is the first of all?' Jesus answered, 'The first is, "Hear, O Israel: The Lord our God, the Lord is one; and you shall love the Lord your God with all your heart, and with all your soul, and with all your mind, and with all your strength." The second is this, "You shall love your neighbor as yourself." There is no other commandment greater than these.' And the scribe said to him, 'You are right, Teacher; you have truly said that he is one, and there is no other but he; and to love him with all the heart, and with all the understanding, and with all the strength, and to love one's neighbor as oneself, is much more than all whole burnt offerings and sacrifices.' And when Jesus saw that he answered wisely, he said to him, 'You are not far from the kingdom of God.' And after that no one dared to ask him any question" (Mark 12:28–34).

"We know that we have crossed the frontier from death to life because we do love our brothers. The man without love for his brother is living in death already. The man who actively hates his brother is a potential murderer, and you will readily see that the eternal life of God cannot live in the heart of a murderer" (I John 3:14–15).

"God is love" (I John 4:15).

"It is this God whom you are worshiping in ignorance that I am here to proclaim to you! God who made the world and all that is in it, being Lord of both Heaven and earth, does not live in temples made by human hands, nor is he ministered to by human hands, as though he had need of anything—seeing that he is the one who gives to all men life and breath and everything else. From one forefather he has created every race of men to live over the face of the whole earth. He has determined the times of their existence and the limits of their habitation, so that they might search for God, in the hope that they might feel for him and find him—yes, even though he is not far from any one of us. Indeed, it is in him that we live and move and have our being" (Acts 17:23–28).

"Lord, thou hast been our dwelling place in all generations" (Psalms 90:1).

"Jehovah appeared of old unto me, saying, yea, I have loved thee with an everlasting love: therefore with loving kindness have I drawn thee" (Jeremiah 31:3).

"I have loved you just as the Father has loved me. You must go on living in my love. If you will keep my commandments you will live in my love just as I have kept my Father's commandments and live in His love. I have told you this so you can share my joy, and that your happiness may be complete. This is my commandment: that you love one another as I have loved you" (John 15:9–12).

The great souls through whom the revelations in our Bible came were no strangers to the truth that God is our dwelling place, that God is love, and that when we awaken to the truth we will live in love.

"And now I will show you the best way of all. I may speak in tongues of men or of angels, but if I am without love, I am a sounding gong or a clanging cymbal. I may have the gift of prophecy, and know every hidden truth; I may have faith strong enough to move mountains; but if I have no love, I am nothing. I may dole out all I possess, or even give my body to be burnt, but if I have no love, I am none the better. Love is patient; love is kind and envies no one. Love is never boastful, nor conceited, nor rude; never selfish, not quick to take offence. Love keeps no score of wrongs; does not gloat over other men's sins, but delights in the truth. There is nothing love cannot face; there is no limit to its faith, its hope, and its endurance. Love will never come to an end. Are there prophets? their work will be over. Are there tongues of ecstasy? they will cease. Is there knowledge? it will vanish away; for our knowledge and our prophecy alike are partial, and the partial vanishes when wholeness comes. When I was a child, my speech, my outlook, and my thoughts were all childish. When I grew up, I had finished with childish things. Now we see only puzzling reflections in a mirror, but then we shall see face to face. My knowledge now is partial; then it will be whole, like God's knowledge of me. In a word, there are three things that last for ever: faith, hope, and love; but the greatest of them all is love. Put love first" (I Corinthians 12:31, 13:1–13, 14:1).

"And anyone who looks down on his brother as a lost soul is himself heading straight for the fire of destruction" (Matthew 5:22).

"Let us leave behind the elementary teaching about Christ and go forward to adult understanding. Let us not lay over and over again the foundation truths—repentance from the deeds which led to death, believing in God, baptism and laying on of hands, belief in the life to come and the final judgment. No, if God allows, let us go on" (Hebrews 6:1).

"The whole creation is on tiptoe to see the wonderful sight of the sons of God coming into their own. The world of creation cannot as yet see reality, not because it chooses to be blind, but because in God's purpose it has been so limited—yet it has been given hope. And the hope is that in the end the whole of created life will be rescued from the tyranny of change and decay, and have its share in that magnificent liberty which can only belong to the children of God" (Romans 8:19–21).

"But someone has said:
What is man, that thou art mindful of him?
Or the son of man, that thou visitest him?
Thou madest him a little lower than the angels;
Thou crownedst him with glory and honor,
And didst set him over the works of thy hands;
Thou didst put all things in subjection under his feet.
Notice that the writer puts 'all things' under the sovereignty of man: he left nothing outside his control. But we do not yet see 'all things' under his control" (Hebrews 2:6–8).

"Once again the Jews picked up stones to stone him. At this Jesus said to them, 'I have set before you many good deeds, done by my Father's power; for which of these would you stone me?' The Jews replied, 'We are not going to stone you for any good deed, but for your blasphemy. You, a mere man, claim to be a god.' Jesus answered: 'Is it not written in your own Law, "I said: You are gods"? Those are called gods to whom the word of God was delivered—and Scripture cannot be set aside. Then why do you charge me with blasphemy because I, consecrated and sent into the world by the Father, said, "I am God's son"?

"'If I am not acting as my Father would, do not believe me. But if I am, accept the evidence of my deeds, even if you do not believe me, so that you may recognize and know that the Father is in me, and I in the Father'" (John 10:31–38).

"If anyone wishes to be a follower of mine, he must leave self behind; he must take up his cross and come with me. Whoever cares for his own safety is lost; but if a man will let himself be lost for my sake, he will find his true self. What will a man gain by winning the whole world, at the cost of his true self? Or what can he give that will buy that self back? For the Son of Man is to come in the glory of his Father with his angels, and then he will give each man the due reward for what he has done. I tell you this: There are some standing here who will not taste death before they have seen the Son of Man coming in his kingdom" (Matthew 16:24–28, NEB).

"So our love for him grows more and more, filling us with complete confidence for the day when he shall judge all men—for we realize that our life in this world is actually his life lived in us" (I John 4:17).

"The kingdom of God (Love) is like a man scattering seed on the ground and then going to bed each night and getting up every morning, while the seed sprouts and grows up, though he has no idea how it happens. The earth produces a crop without any help from anyone: first a blade, then the ear of corn, then the full-grown grain in the ear" (Mark 4:26–28, Phillips).

"Consider the incredible love that the Father has shown us in allowing us to be called 'children of God'—and that is not just what we are called, but what we are. Our heredity on the God-ward side is no mere figure of speech—which explains why the world will no more recognize us than it recognized Christ. Here and now we are God's children. We don't know what we shall become in the future. We only know that if reality were to break through, we should reflect his likeness, for we should see him as he really is! Everyone who has at heart a hope like that keeps himself pure, for he knows how pure Christ is" (I John 3:1–3).

"I will give the victorious some of the hidden manna, and I will also give him a white stone with a new name written upon it which no man knows except the man who receives it" (Revelation 2:17).

"Turning to the Jews who had believed him, Jesus said, 'If you dwell within the revelation I have brought, you are indeed my disciples; you shall know the truth and the truth will set you free.' They replied, 'We are Abraham's descendants; we have never been in slavery to any man. What do you mean by saying "You will become free men"?' 'In very truth I tell you,' said Jesus, 'that everyone who commits sin is a slave. The slave has no permanent standing in the household, but the son belongs to it for ever. If then the Son sets you free, you will indeed be free!'" (John 8:31–36, NEB).

"O Christ, Thou Son of God,
My own eternal self;
Live Thou Thy life in me,
Do Thou Thy will in me,
Be Thou made flesh in me.
I will have no will but Thine,
I will have no self but Thee."

(Gaelic Prayer)

## HEAVEN * * * * SURPRISE

I dreamt death came, the other night,
And Heaven's gate swung wide.
An Angel with a halo bright,
Ushered me inside.

And there! to my astonishment,
Stood folks I'd judged and labeled
As "quite unfit," "of little worth,"
And "spiritually disabled!"

Indignant words rose to my lips,
But never were set free,
For every face showed stunned surprise—
Not one expected me.

(Author Unknown)

REMINDERS

## ON CREATIVITY

"The man who follows the crowd will usually get no further than the crowd. The man who walks alone is likely to find himself in places no one has ever been before.

"Creativity in living is not without its attendant difficulties, for peculiarity breeds contempt. And the unfortunate thing about being ahead of your time is that when people finally realize you were right, they'll say it was obvious all along.

"You have two choices in life: you can dissolve into the mainstream, or you can be distinct. To be distinct, you must be different. To be different, you must strive to be what no one else but you can be."

(Alan Ashley-Pitt)

## OUTWITTED

He drew a circle that shut me out—
Heretic, rebel, a thing to flout.
But Love and I had the wit to win;
We drew a circle that took him in!

(Edwin Markham)

Love acts; fear reacts.

Love acts out of the riches of its own nature. Fear reacts out of the poverty of its nature.

Love is more than "horsetrading" in affection. Love is the creative energy that runs the whole universe.

Love makes all things new. It never insists that we stay where we are, but only that we start there.

When we wake up in love, we stop trying to love everyone equally, and begin the delightful assignment of loving each one uniquely.

Rejoice in the love that reveals yourself to you.

Be delighted by the love that makes you sure of your true identity.

Praise the love that fulfills your desire to know yourself.

Happiness comes from the deep understanding and appreciation of oneself. When a person has attained this, then the happiness is strong enough to flow into any relationship and become a vital part of it.

Love yourself alive!

## XXVII

## IT IS FINISHED!

Just as authors don't really write books, they write themselves—so readers don't really read books, they read themselves. Perhaps, then, since I had to write this book, you, in a certain sense, *had to read it!* Or at least, you read it. In the long and deep look of love, there are no accidents. Love has its own life processes of awakening all of us to the truth that we are its self-expression—unique creatures of infinite potential. Somewhere along the eternal path of love, life, light, and laughter we realize with deepening gratitude and all due humility (but no more) that our search for selfhood is over, it has come to an end, it is finished! Perhaps something you have read in this book has brought you to this realization. Perhaps some person in your world has said: "I have the feeling that you have found yourself. Many people talk about it, but I feel something rare and subtle in you that makes me feel you have found something that most of us are still just talking about." Perhaps out of those long quiet stretches of your soul the inner voice has spoken and told you: "Your search for yourself is over; it is done—it is finished!" This realization may come in other ways, too, of course. You may realize that more and more you are doing your own thinking and feeling. You are no longer struggling so hard to conform or rebel. You are no longer so apprehensive about pleasing or displeasing people. You are no longer so pressured by "labels." You are willing to look with growing love, joy, and confidence at any area of life of your inner being and of human experience. You are finding your own answers to questions such as "Who am I?" "What am I doing?" "Where am I going?"

## HOW TO LOVE YOUR NEIGHBOR

You find that you are no longer so judgmental. You do not feel it is necessary to pass critical judgment on everyone and everything. Rather, you have a growing ability to understand that in every person, every experience, every relationship the Infinite Spirit of love, life, light, and laughter is finding individual expression and is working out creative, fulfilling good for everyone involved. You are more ready to forgive yourself and others, and you are more capable of forgiving in creative, dynamic, and adventurous ways. You can look back into your past experience and have a deep feeling of gratitude for all persons, experiences, and relationships that have been part of your own growth and unfoldment, as you have been of theirs. You can look at your present world, your present relationships, your present opportunities, your present challenges, even your present hangups, with a deep underlying feeling of gratitude, knowing that these, too, are a vital part of your ongrowing path of eternal life, as you are of theirs. You can look gratefully into the future, knowing that you will continue to experience more of what you really are, more of what the Infinite Spirit of the universe is, more of what your neighbor truly is. You will be catching at least occasional glimpses of the eternal dimensions of being—your own and your neighbors'.

You will realize more and more, and it will probably come as a feeling rather than an intellectual concept, that you are a vital part of all that is. You will feel your oneness with God and with your neighbor. In a very real sense, the whole universe will be your neighbor and you will feel your growing oneness with all its creatures.

You will become more deeply conscious of the mighty L-current of love, life, light, and laughter within you and within your neighbor. You will be increasingly loyal to the spiritual dimensions of being; more willing to surrender to them, be receptive to them, become them; more grateful for the liberty and freedom that stir within you and within everyone who comes into your life.

You will become more expert in converting the mighty L-current into a laser beam of creative energy that operates within yourself and within your world. As old feelings of limitation, imitation, frustration, resentment, or unhappiness come out of the depths of your subconscious mind, you will be able to direct that laser beam of love, life, light, and laughter at them, declaring for each one: "Thank you, Infinite Spirit of love. This old state is over. It is done. It is finished!" Perhaps, like a friend of mine, you will decide to have a cremation service each evening, in which you consciously consign old states of limitation to the fire of purification that burns forever to take care of the remnants of the devil and his angels (the outgrown patterns, habits, and inhibitions of the past). You will realize that old memories, experiences, and challenges that used to unbutton you mentally and emotionally can now be laughed out of your consciousness, and you'll have many an inner chuckle as the mighty L-current frees you to be a more creative, dynamic, and adventurous partner in every relationship you share.

More and more you will be a Spiritual Independent in practice as well as in potential. You will realize that you have not reached any final destination, that there is no reason for you to pat yourself on the back, because you have an infinite path to travel. On the other hand, you will be through with much false humility and be willing to accept and appreciate the progress that is being made in your own self-unfoldment, because you will realize that you are the handiwork of the infinite Creative Spirit that has never forsaken you and never will.

You will realize that no one else is going to be responsible for your own selfhood. You are created to be the unique, unduplicatable, indestructible self-expression of the infinite Creative Spirit of the universe—and you have accepted self-responsibility. More and more you will be meeting Spiritual Independents wherever you are. Young or old, male or female, all colors, rich or poor, playing or working—you will know each other from the impact of a glance, from the tone of voice, or the throbbing, vibrant silence between you, or the feel of a creative surge of the laser beam of love, life, light, and laughter that you exchange in the space of a heartbeat. You will know and be known. If you were to put your realization of selfhood into words, perhaps they would come out something like this: *"My search for myself is over, it is ended, it is finished! With deepening gratitude and all due humility, but no more, I realize that I have found myself. I recognize that the search and the finding and the acceptance are all the work of the universal Creative Spirit of love, life, light, and laughter whose self-expression I am. I am glad that no one else can take on the project of my own selfhood. With growing love, joy, confidence, and enthusiasm I move ahead on the path of spiritual independence. I rejoice every time I feel the impact of another awakening soul in my consciousness."*

You are a fantastic member of the fantastic human family. Drop your crutches. Stand up on your spiritual feet. Love your neighbor and yourself! It is finished!